TEAM TEACHING

The Northern Nevada Writing Project Teacher-Researcher Group

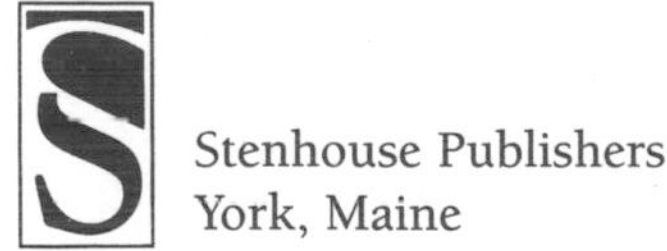

Stenhouse Publishers
York, Maine

Members of the Northern Nevada Writing Project Teacher-Researcher Group

Gaylyn Anderson
Michael Gazaway
Carol Harriman
Tamara Durbin Higgins
Margaret Hill
Elizabeth Knott
Deborah Loesch-Griffin
Susan Martin
Karen McGee
Joan Taylor
Fran Terras
Ellen Williams

Stenhouse Publishers

The research on which this book is based was funded in part by a generous grant from the Walter S. Johnson Foundation of Menlo Park, California.

Library of Congress Cataloging-in-Publication Data
Team teaching / the Northern Nevada Writing Project Teacher-Researcher Group.
p. cm.
ISBN 1-57110-040-7 (alk. paper)
1. Teaching teams—Nevada. 2. Classroom management—Nevada.
I. Northern Nevada Writing Project Teacher-Researcher Group.
LB1029.T4T42 1996
371.1'48—dc20 96-27862
CIP

Cover and interior design by Martha Drury
Manufactured in the United States of America on acid-free paper
03 02 01 00 9 8 7 6 5 4 3 2

CONTENTS

FOREWORD

During the long and rather illustrious history of team teaching, many texts have been prepared in an effort to illuminate the perils and possibilities of collaborative teaching arrangements. Some have offered us data on the approximate number of schools engaged in various forms of team teaching. Other quantitative studies have revealed the dividends of team teaching with regard to teacher efficacy, student attitudes, student discipline, instructional creativity, teacher satisfaction, and empowerment. Still other works have articulated guidelines and procedures for organizing, operating, sustaining, and evaluating team teaching. While many of these rather well-referenced contributions have drawn extensively on the actual experiences of teachers, principals, students, and parents who have lived team teaching, none has captured the inside, teacher voice as surely as this text.

This is a desperately needed work, but not for obvious reasons. After all, attention to the concept of team teaching is not new to the educational community. For the past two decades, support for team teaching has been at the forefront of reform recommendations. Upon the completion of his monumental eight year study, Goodlad (1984) concluded that both elementary and secondary schools needed to seriously reevaluate the presumed advantages of both the self-contained classroom and departmentalization, calling for more intimate and flexible approaches to meeting students' needs, diversified instructional experiences, increased teacher autonomy, and teacher collaboration.

The middle school movement has played a monumental role in cultivating the growth of teaching teams. Literally thousands of middle level schools have reorganized from teaching departments into interdisciplinary teaching teams during the movement's forty-year history. In the 1990s, interdisciplinary teaming has been noted as the signature of the middle school movement (Dickinson and Erb in press), and no doubt one of its most poignant reform contributions.

In the face of increasingly complex classroom situations, many teachers have echoed Goodlad, bemoaning their isolation and yearning for more support and collegiality than either their self-contained or departmentalized settings provide. Furthermore, in light of the collaborative demands suggested by national initiatives such as collaborative special education inclusion, and curriculum integration, many schools are seeking alternatives to the lone-ranger model of teaching so familiar to many schools.

American high school teachers who find themselves in the midst of current reform initiatives such as block scheduling or interdisciplinary instruction, are likewise inclined to examine collaborative ways to enhance curriculum and instruction by merging fields of study and instructional strengths into fashionable new courses. As noted in *Breaking Ranks* (Dickinson and Erb 1996), high school educators are increasingly convinced that single-subject, single-teacher teaching is simply no match for the phenomenal knowledge overload and challenging school situations they are sure to sustain in the decades ahead.

While there is widespread interest in team teaching, there is reason to believe that many existing teaching teams are not thriving. Far too many remain paralyzed by unresolved interpersonal struggles, philosophical divisions or difficulty with the change from the "I" to "we" paradigm. Most of these teams were established with little attention to the inside perils of collaboration. How grand that this text, which works to unearth the internal mysteries of team life, and offer wisdom for its sustenance, has arrived in time to salvage many teams from despair and desertion.

The realization that we must understand teaming beyond its structural features has indeed served to redirect our eye to the intensely interpersonal nature of collaborative teaching. Abundant advice on constructing agendas, structuring meetings, planning interdisciplinary units, creating common class rules, and so on has not embraced the deeper issues of teamwork with pose the greatest threat to the gifts of the educational construct. Difference is the beginning of synergy or the end, but which depends on the dynamics between persons who must weave that fabric of synergy together.

This book is the first of its kind to embrace the pervasive issues of team teaching. In search of truth about how best to team teach, committed teachers decided to search for answers in their very own schools and classrooms. Numbers aside, they studied stories from teachers, parents, students, and principals who ventured to participate in team teaching. From these stories, they gathered a portrait of the often unspoken struggles and triumphs, the hopes and heartaches, and the dreams and dilemmas that can accompany the team teaching endeavor.

There is no hiding behind jargon or snappy formulas here. This text exposes with startling honesty the sheer terror of unveiling one's teacher identity to another, the pain of losing a successful teammate, the tension created by differing needs for order and quiet, the agony of leading teams, the frustration in finding common ground in philosophy and purpose, and the humility, professionalism, joy and pride that can grow in a productive team relationship. It might have been enough to have simply shared the rich and descriptive experiences included here, but the text takes us beyond the tales into truths that have perennial merit in the world of practice. It is a remarkable blend of heart and hand.

It seems clear that the authors have achieved their hope of producing a work that offered more than data to support team teaching; they have delivered an inspiring guide to help teachers map a team teaching journey with promising landmarks and informative roadside markers. What's most rewarding about this contribution, however, is its authenticity of sentiment, purpose, and content. It is not beguiled by persuasive language. Instead, it is a well analyzed account of the real thing and as such is a rare gift to the educational community.

Nancy M. Doda

Dickinson, T., and T. Erb, eds. In press. *We Gain More Than We Give: Teaming in the Middle School*. Columbus, OH: National Middle School Association.

———. 1996. *Breaking Ranks: Changing an American Institution*. Reston, VA: NASSP.

Goodlad, J. 1984. *A Place Called School*. New York: McGraw.

ACKNOWLEDGMENTS

I am honored to thank a group of people who put their best efforts into this research project and resulting book. Each member enriched and enhanced the product, but what stands out is the way each person enriched and enhanced the process and our journey together.

Gaylyn Anderson, Mike Gazaway, Carol Harriman, Margaret Hill, Liz Knott, Debby Loesch-Griffin, Sue Martin, Karen McGee, Joan Taylor, Fran Terras, Ellen Williams, and I worked together for three years, meeting on the second and fourth Tuesdays of each month. My colleagues never shirked their duties, and they maintained a sense of humor throughout. It's been a privilege and a pleasure to work with such dynamic and gifted professionals.

Once the drafts of all chapters were completed, Gaylyn Anderson began an intensive editing process. Her meticulous pen has strengthened the book immeasurably: she refused to be satisfied with material that was "just OK."

Working with us from day one, our assistant, Cheryl Davis, kept us on track. She helped solve technical problems and knew how to make us look good. Without her help, support, and hand-holding, our book would still be papers in file folders.

Kudos to all the team teachers and principals in Washoe County, Nevada, who supported our study with time, information, and professionalism. This book is truly for them. We have given them pseudonyms, but we are sure they will all recognize themselves as they read the book.

Our deep gratitude to the Walter S. Johnson Foundation of Menlo Park, California. Our primary contact, Kim Ford, helped facilitate the grant application process and our subsequent study.

To Bob Tierney, Marian Mohr, Faye Reitgmans, Carol Jago, and Judith Shulman we extend great appreciation for their training and guidance as teacher researchers.

We would also like to thank Mary Nebgen for supporting this project. She allowed us to apply for a grant through the Washoe County School District, thereby giving us the nonprofit status we needed. Her ongoing encouragement helped, too.

To our families, our heartfelt thanks for your patience, support, response, editing, and love! Your help enabled us to produce a book. We couldn't have done it without you.

This book began with a question, and we realize that our answers are not all-inclusive. What we do know is that we are better teachers and researchers because of our experiences together. We hope that you enjoy reading about our odyssey and that you ask some new questions yourself. If you do, our task is complete.

Tamara Durbin Higgins

INTRODUCTION

Teacher-researcher groups are typically composed of educators who want to identify issues and find solutions to the problems they face every day in their own classrooms, in their schools, and in the educational system. We, the members of the Northern Nevada Writing Project (NNWP) Teacher-Researcher Group, have been together since 1988. Each year we choose a new project (or continue with an unfinished one) and work together to give one another both feedback and support. Research coupled with full-time teaching is very demanding, both mentally and physically. However, we generally agree that the dialogue that goes on during our alternate Tuesday afternoon seminars encourages us to keep on going with our projects and spurs us on to ask new questions, seek new solutions, and continue to evolve as professionals.

In the fall of 1990 the Nevada state legislature mandated a fifteen-to-one student-teacher ratio for all first-grade classes. Because of space limitations, districts statewide were able to fulfill the mandate only by forming teams—two teachers in one classroom with thirty students. The mandate also called for a sixteen-to-one ratio in the second grade in the fall of 1991, to be followed by a sixteen-to-one ratio in the third grade starting in 1992. Several members of our group were already members of a teaching team in 1990, and more would find themselves team teaching in the following two years.

Although the district made genuine efforts to orient teachers to team teaching, very little literature was available to district personnel to help them develop a structure for training teachers or administrators in dealing with this new teaching arrangement. Team teaching was neither well understood nor well documented. We felt that a widespread study of team teaching would be beneficial, and so decided to undertake such a project.

Our research continued over a three-year period, and the results are presented in the chapters that follow. Appendix A contains a detailed discussion of our methodology.

We went into this study thinking many things, holding several assumptions. Among them was the notion that we would find experts who could direct us and that after a certain prescribed set of studying research procedures and collecting data, we would nail down team teaching. If any barriers were broken as the result of our work, it was the compulsion to circumscribe team teaching and to say that all things within that boundary were characteristic of team teaching, and all things outside it were not.

One of our most startling findings is that team teachers themselves are the best judges of what circumstances will and will not work for them, and as a result, this book is intended to be descriptive, not prescriptive. We hope the stories we present will provide a multitude of possibilities, will serve as a beginning point rather than an evaluation tool.

Finally, we want this book to be a resource and a comfort for those teachers embarking on a new teaching journey—one that is challenging yet holds the potential for the finest professional fulfillment.

I am at the blackboard going over vocabulary from a story that we're doing in class. On this particular day, I'm not feeling exceptionally bright, nor am I feeling particularly obtuse. But for some reason, I can't think of a way to illustrate the word *phenomenon*. As an ESL teacher, I am constantly searching for ways to demonstrate concepts graphically, not just depend on verbalizing. This one is more than I can manage today. Finally, in desperation, I turn to my partner (why didn't I think of this earlier?):

> *Me:* Ms. K., can you think of an example that would help the class understand what *phenomenon* means?
>
> *Ms. K:* Boys and girls, if my desk were suddenly to appear before you in a neat and organized manner, that would be a *phenomenon*.

The children nod with understanding. I nod with relief and go on to the next challenge.

How do people teach alone? What do you do when you can't think of how to explain a concept and you're at the board with twenty-five children looking at you? What do you do when you're really stumped—when your brain can't give you an answer on the spot? I rely on my partner to come through. Yes, I'll admit it. I'm addicted to team teaching.

Rita Marschall
Fourth-Fifth-Sixth-Grade Elementary Teacher

CHAPTER 1

Team Teaching Configurations

Mentioning the term *team teaching* is very much like saying *house* or *dog* or *child*. We all form a different picture in our heads depending on our experience and perspective. The configuration of teams does, in fact, look very different across grade levels and even within particular grades. Often the configuration is dictated by the reasons for the team's formation in the first place.

As we explored the various teams in our study, we realized that defining team teaching can be difficult. (For details of how we conducted our study and the number and kinds of classrooms we considered, see Chapter 2 and Appendix A.) Some teachers share only physical space; they do not plan together, nor do their classes exist as a single unit. Other teachers plan together and coordinate activities and curriculum, but are never together in the same classroom at the same time. Are both of these configurations team teaching? We allowed the teachers in our study to determine if they saw themselves as members of a team. If they did, then so did we. As one teacher said in an interview, "Because everyone is different, it's interesting how all teams are different. Their set-ups are different, their approaches are different, their daily schedules are different, yet they are all hired to do the same thing."

Teams in the Elementary Schools

Team teaching in Nevada elementary schools would appear to be natural: two teachers share approximately thirty students in the same room all day. However, the manner in which the teams function together in the classroom can be very different.

Dividing the Students/Dividing the Teaching Time

A few elementary teams in our study literally divided the room in half with a physical partition. Each teacher had his or her own fifteen students. In such cases, the team shared the physical space but did not teach together, though issues such as discipline had to be addressed by both teachers.

This arrangement did not necessarily preclude sharing students. One team in our survey divided subjects as well as the room. Each member of this team taught certain subjects to all the students, but fifteen at a time. Each taught her strong subjects: Helen taught math, for example, while her partner taught handwriting. One team teacher who taught in a room where the subject matter had been divided after some unsuccessful attempts at whole-group work commented in her journal:

> We started our new system this week and it was wonderful. This finally feels like what team teaching should be: both of us working with small groups of kids. We still do several things as a class—art, P.E., spelling—but the prime learning time is more personal now.

Some teams divided the teaching time instead of partitioning the room. Denise explained that she taught from 9:30 to 11:30 A.M. and her partner from 11:30 A.M. to 2:00 P.M. Each was in charge of a different major curricular area each week, and whoever was in charge of the current science or social studies unit would teach from 2:00 until 3:00 P.M. Structures such as these alleviated the need for team members to spend a great deal of time planning together.

Whole Groups/Small Groups/Centers

We found that the majority of the teams in our study used a more eclectic approach than simply dividing the room or the teaching in half. Instead, they broke the day into different teaching/learning situations. The day might begin with one teacher teaching a whole-group lesson. Whole-group work usually involved all of the students and both teachers working on the same thing at the same time. For example, one of the teachers of a second-grade team in the process of doing whole-group math commented:

> We've been doing time. So if my partner is doing the presentation up there with the clock, and the kids have their clocks and work sheets at their desks, then I'm floating around with my marker, giving them stars if they're getting [the work] all right. So both of us are almost always on the floor at all times.

Many of our respondents talked about this approach, where one teacher teaches while the other uses a different method to reinforce the same material. Others taught simultaneously, playing off each other in front of the whole group, then breaking the class into small groups. Many felt that this approach was the best way to get students involved in their own learning at a very early age. April reflected on this idea in her journal:

> In structuring a class so that children are learning in small groups (from four to six children) there can be more involvement by the child

> in the learning. I think that to sell the team concept you must get teachers to buy into the idea that everyone in the classroom can teach as well as learn.

Small-group work was often followed by students going to various centers throughout the room. Gladys mentioned that the centers are often staffed by parent helpers as well as teachers. Here's a typical description:

> One of us is working with six children in reading and six children in writing, and the other person is working with six children in math and six children in word study. We go back and forth between those groups working, with the follow-through. We have a parent volunteer here in a fifth center every day.

This kind of flexible approach allowed the teachers to teach all the subject areas in the curriculum, but required more planning time on the part of the teams.

Team-Taught Multilevel Classrooms

Many schools experimented with classes of two or three grade levels in one self-contained classroom. Clara and Renée taught a combined first and second grade. They made no special allowances for the two age groups. All their small groups were heterogeneous, and the groups did not necessarily remain the same throughout the year. Language arts was taught using centers, four groups rotating between seat work, writing workshop, literature study, and word study in roughly twenty-minute intervals. For other subjects, such as math, the whole group worked together.

A first-second-third-grade combination did roughly this same rotation, but during a whole-group lesson, the team members would alternate, sometimes in five-minute intervals, so that both teachers were always teaching everything. The students in this classroom, like those in the combined first- and second-grade classroom, were also ability grouped regardless of age or grade level. Norma and her partner made one concession for the first graders to give them extra reading practice: the second and third graders read to each other in groups, but the first graders read to each other and to the teachers, other students, and parents.

Teams for Special-Needs Students

Conventional wisdom in education these days rejects the idea that a student with special needs should be removed from the classroom for extra help in a pull-out program; rather, that student should receive whatever special help is needed within the context of the regular classroom. In such a "push-in" program, a specialist divides his or her day among several classrooms, teaming with teachers to help students with special needs, such as English as a Second Language (ESL) students and remedial readers.

Barbara, a special-education teacher, pushed in four different upper-elementary classrooms (fourth, fifth, and sixth grades) for at least one hour each day. In three of the four classes, she was in on the planning in reading and math, and the classroom teachers helped write the individual education plans, which, Barbara said, made the documents more valid than they otherwise would have been. In the fourth classroom, Barbara planned for her special needs students independently and worked with them in a small group. Barbara felt that the strength of team teaching in these situations was the flexibility in planning and collaborating with the regular teaching staff.

Katherine, a remedial reading teacher, also pushed in four regular classrooms every day, supporting the reading program and, in some cases, the entire language arts curriculum in those classes. The regular classroom teacher scheduled her reading period to accommodate Katherine's schedule. Together Katherine and the regular teacher planned, evaluated, tested, and adapted the curriculum to meet the needs of the remedial students in language arts. The students were allowed to participate in the regular classroom experiences at their own level.

At another school an ESL teacher taught with a fifth-grade teacher for seventy-five minutes a day so that her second-language students could remain in the regular classroom. The ESL students who needed the most help were assigned to that fifth-grade class. The ESL teacher and the classroom teacher planned together and cotaught the class during that period. The program has recently been expanded to the sixth grade, where the ESL teacher teams with the regular teachers for units in social studies, science, and math.

Team teaching to help special-needs students succeed in the regular classroom is not unique to the elementary grades. Four of the high school teachers in our survey taught in a team situation involving a special-education teacher and a teacher in a curricular area. Typically, the team worked together for one class daily.

June and Bea formed a team after the school year had started to teach a freshman English class. June brought ten special-education students into Bea's regular English class. At first, Bea took the lead teaching the material, while June worked in a support capacity, but as the team progressed, both planned the lessons and shared in the teaching responsibilities. (Another special-education teacher teamed in a math class in this same way.)

At another high school, an ESL teacher teamed with a special-education teacher for one period. The idea in this case was to offer the freshmen an extra step before entering regular English classes because so many ESL and special-education students were failing freshman English.

In all these cases, the participants felt that each teacher grew from the team experience. The special-education teachers gained a better knowledge of the subject matter, and the regular classroom teacher learned how to slow down and to be more thorough in covering material. One special-education teacher described her experience like this:

> If you put children in homogeneous situations, they are going to imitate those behaviors. All they are doing is reinforcing each other's disabilities, and I don't feel it's healthy. The thing I found out was what an enabler I was to a special-education student. Working with a regular classroom teacher, I found out that I was helping them too much, that I needed to put a lot more responsibility back on the student.

This sentiment was echoed by every secondary special-education teacher in our study.

Teams in Middle Schools and High Schools

Team teachers often compare themselves to marriage partners. To extend the metaphor, if elementary teams could be seen as married, the teams in middle schools and high schools might more accurately be described as just dating: they teach together for one or two class periods, not the whole day.

Another major difference between elementary and high school teams is that the latter were usually voluntary: teachers in different disciplines sought out a partner from another discipline to offer an interdisciplinary class—usually sixty students for a two-hour block. Being able to synthesize information for students in the two disciplines was the primary purpose of the class. Too often, because the day is broken into periods, middle and high school students' education is fragmented. Interdisciplinary classes help students see the relationships between disciplines, assuring that they make connections they would otherwise be left to make on their own.

Mavis and Martha taught a sophomore honors class, World Cultures, which met for two hours in the afternoon. The two-hour block offered a variety of teaching configurations. On some days, each teacher led the class in her discipline for an hour, while the other played a support role. If the class was involved in a special project, both hours were devoted to that project. The class spent a great deal of time working in small groups with both teachers moving from group to group. Both teachers felt that even with sixty students, the small groups and the flexibility of a two-hour block contributed to a sense of community they did not find in their other classes.

Rhea was the English teacher of a similar class, American Studies. Because of the physical limitations of the school, the class of sixty students could never meet at the same time. Each teacher taught American Studies for one hour each day. The two would plan and coordinate the lessons, but they never actually taught together. Often, Rhea would sit in on the social studies hour because it was during her preparation period, but she seldom, if ever, did anything but observe.

In a similar middle school class two teachers shared a two-hour English and social studies block. Some days they met whole class and some days they divided the group into two sections. Both Joyce and Valerie believed in a student-centered classroom, so they had many workshops. When they lectured, they alternated. Joyce explained, "If we were going to introduce a unit we might both take a voice in a poem to show how it is done. I might introduce something and then do a little dance shuffle and say, 'OK, partner, you're on,' and so we alternated."

A new middle school in our district allowed larger groups to form. Seventy to a hundred students could meet in one room. They were divided into large groups and given separate identities: team names, cheers, and mottoes. Each group was taught by an interdisciplinary core team of three teachers who taught the basic subjects—English, social studies, and science. The three-person team was augmented by other teachers who taught electives, such as life skills, technology, and physical education. For the majority of class time, one teacher still taught a subject to a regular-sized class. The difference was that the seven-member (three core and four elective) teaching team coordinated the curriculum, the homework, and the discipline policies of the whole student team.

The student teams met in team rooms at least once a week, more often if they were involved in a large-group project. During the other times the team teachers could manipulate the time spent in each class; for example, the science teacher could be given more time on a given day for a particular lesson.

Once a month, the extended core team of seven met to resolve student and curricular problems. The flexibility of this core teachers–core students setup allowed teachers to be creative in their lesson plans. And because they shared a particular group of students, these teachers could help the students more effectively if they began to falter in any curricular area.

Team Teaching Variations

From just the few examples given in this chapter, it's obvious that team teaching can look very different from level to level and class to class. Even interschool configurations are possible. A teacher at one school can team with a teacher at another school to do particular units. It was not uncommon for a high school teacher in our study to team with an elementary teacher and have the classes write back and forth to each other. Rhoda and Marnie, for example, teamed first graders and high schoolers. The first graders wrote letters to Santa, and the high schoolers responded. Sometimes the high school students wrote children's stories and then went to the elementary classroom to present them to the students.

Nedra, a fifth-grade teacher in a high socioeconomic area, teamed with a fifth-grade teacher across town in a low socioeconomic area. The students in the two classes wrote back and forth and got together for picnics on their own time. Part of the reason these teachers brought the classes together was so that their students could get to know different kinds of people.

One of the high school teachers in our study expanded the definition of team teaching even further. She envisioned an entire faculty coming together for a "mass teaming situation." She has begun work on an idea for a schoolwide morning news show to be shown in all of the classrooms. The news program would involve every discipline on campus, with all teachers contributing to the content, design, plan, and follow-up.

Given the variations we encountered in our study, perhaps the best definition of team teaching is a broad one: two or more teachers coming together for a common purpose to help enhance their teaching and their students' learning.

The first day of my first real, contracted school year I was a little nervous and also feeling very grown up in my official teacher role. This position at this school had been my ultimate career goal. I had been offered positions at other schools, but I held out, and miraculously my dream job was realized.

I met my partner at my interview, and we spent two months preparing for our first year. We became friends as well as colleagues. I felt fortunate that someone with ten years' experience was flexible enough to take me in as a partner. Even with all the time we spent together previously, I was not prepared on that first day to see Sonia interact with the children. The door shut and suddenly this woman transformed into Super Teacher! She spoke so lovingly and memorized each of the thirty-one children's names so quickly! I felt so awkward, like an imposter. Who was I to think I could accept the title "teacher"? She was so calm and sincere. The children adored her. I wanted to cry, to run away, just to not have to compare my feeble attempts with her grace. But more than that, I wanted to be a teacher like her. I wanted to be that good.

If Sonia noticed my fear and apprehension, she graciously ignored it. She treated me as an equal, not always agreeing with me but always encouraging and supporting me. She politely joined in my game of "Let's pretend I'm a teacher too!"

From the beginning Sonia asked my opinions and ideas. I forced myself to make suggestions and share. It was so hard when her fat, fat folders were so full of so many marvelous activities for one school year. My few files were so thin we used one of my file drawers to store paper. And yet Sonia asked for copies of my activities for her files. She also offered hers if I was interested. Was I interested?! What beginning teacher would turn away from such a resource?

Michelle Bassett
First-Grade Teacher

CHAPTER

2

Beginnings

When the Nevada state legislature mandated a ratio of fifteen students to one teacher, it quickly became apparent that some major changes would have to take place, that classes and teachers would have to double up to comply with the law. Individual schools were allowed to determine who would team teach and where their classrooms would be located given the existing facilities.

The most visionary principals helped teachers form teams and subsequently responded to team needs. Professional teacher-training coordinators also scrambled to provide assistance. However, for the most part, teachers were expected to take on the responsibility of collaborating and becoming self-managed, successful teams. They were expected to develop the mutual respect and trust it takes to work together.

First-grade teachers were the first to deal with the challenge. Sherry recalled:

> Partners were told on Thursday they were to combine students on the following Monday. I refused. "Give us at least one week." We were together a week from that Monday. There was no time before school, and [the change] was not funded in any way. We met for two hours while others took our classes.

Cami displayed some positive energy toward the prospect of team teaching:

> We decided we would make this work. You can fight something and be miserable, or you can accept it and find the good. We will find the good. We have different styles of teaching, but I feel we will mesh very well. Also, we said we will not break up our friendship over this. We will communicate with each other.

Forming Teams

During those frantic, frenzied first days of team formation and initial team collaboration, and with the combination of time pressure and outside influences, it was difficult for those involved to make rational, focused decisions. As team teachers reflected on that time with us, most concurred that logical planning and careful choices were often tripped up by politics and fate.

Teachers within their own schools, particularly those who lacked job seniority, began looking for partners with compatible personalities and/or teaching styles. They talked openly with potential partners, with other staff members, with principals, and with significant others. Sara said,

> My partner and I started out last year thinking we would be teaching together, and we did a lot of discussing. Then when we took a trip together to San Francisco, we talked the whole way down and back, and it seemed like we were on the same wavelength in a lot of areas.

A few teachers began looking outside their own schools for partners. They hoped to obtain administrative approval once a possible arrangement had been secured.

Some considered asking friends to become their partners, since they already knew their friends' philosophies and styles of teaching. Margaret said, "I would want to pick someone who was a friend already instead of going in cold turkey with someone I didn't know at all." According to Virginia, "Dealing with a stranger might be easier, but working with a friend, you know what to expect, even if you don't like it." Other teachers decided against teaming with close friends, reasoning that the strain of being partners for at least seven hours a day could jeopardize their friendship. What if they discovered things about each other they couldn't respect?

Sometimes parents suggested possible teaching partners, sometimes counselors or other teachers did. Everyone became a potential matchmaker, knowing "just the right person for you."

In some cases, principals needed to hire team partners. Some did so unilaterally; others invited current staff members to be present during the interviews, either as silent observers or as participants. As several of our interviewees reflected on the selection process, they felt the partner-to-be of the new hire should insist on being present at the interview. Faye said, "I'd want to be in on the interview, especially if I was there first and they were bringing someone in to me. I'd want to be in on the interview and hear their answers."

Shannon extended that thought. "I'd like to interview them two or three times, not just a first time, because that first time they're always trying to be good. The second time you might really see what they're like." She said she would ask, "If you have report cards due to the principal on Wednesday morning and it's Friday afternoon and you and I are both going to be busy all weekend, would you be willing to stay Monday and Tuesday to get those report cards done?"

Dale warned about posing leading questions during an interview. "People are just as glib as they have always been. Some people give you the answers you want to hear."

Even though Angela had interviewed her current partner, it didn't work out. The next time in an interview, she plans to ask questions about classroom management, use of space, and planning strategies. "I would also like to know if they are flexible or structured. I feel that they should ask questions about me, too."

Teachers were also teamed up by chance: straws were drawn, names were put into a hat, and winners or losers, depending on your point of view, became a team.

Finding the Ideal Partner

If you accept the fact that no one is perfect, then the perfect teammate is not only elusive but nonexistent. Nevertheless, team teachers in our study had some definite ideas about who their ideal partner might be. Philosophies, classroom environments, methods of discipline, and personality types were their main concerns.

"How would I choose a new partner?" Shannon reiterated the question.

> I'd have to sit down and really think about what I'd want to ask them. I'd like to interview them, go to lunch with them, then probably go to dinner with them, and then probably have breakfast with them, and probably never choose them because I honestly can't think of replacing my partner now. If she died tomorrow, I'd be in trouble. I'd probably try to get a single room. Even though my principal matched me with my partner, I don't trust that he could do that again. He just got lucky.

Phyllis said she would easily recognize her ideal partner:

> You know right off the bat. You could go into a school and sit with people and just listen and hear how they talk, see if they're tired and sick of their job and don't like children.

Virginia was concerned with less threatening issues, such as classroom arrangement. She would ask, "Does she use centers? Does she like to have easels in her room? Does she like hands-on math?" Along similar lines, Pearl wanted to know whether the prospective partner prefers desks to tables.

Educational Philosophy

Sally felt that thinking about and articulating one's educational philosophy was especially important when the person was part of a team. Several respondents mentioned the need to have compatible philosophies, and some teachers specifically felt they needed to know whether a potential partner's teaching would be predominantly child-centered or curriculum-centered.

"I would look for a philosophy similar to mine," Eileen stated. "The way they teach isn't exactly it. Somebody who sees kids the way I do is closer. I would want their expectation level of kids to be similar to mine." Shannon said, "We should try to have a common goal: probably, it's teach the children as best we can, in the time that we're allowed, and have a good time."

Sonia said that partners would need to see eye to eye on their teaching methods and philosophies: how they group their students in reading or how they integrate a new child into the classroom. Gayle focused on methods of teaching reading and math; to her, these areas were the most important in first grade. Sara liked having a lot of books in the room and would like a partner who shared this desire. She felt there should be all sorts of books available and the students should have an opportunity to choose their own books. She would also look for a person who felt that writing is an integral part of learning. Jill said that three concepts would be important to her in assessing a potential partner: educational philosophy of whole language versus phonics strategies; expectations of students; and teaching styles.

Renée mentioned these same three ideas more specifically: "I would hope that she was whole language [oriented] and that she had a developmental view of children as opposed to a skills-oriented view."

Twyla was concerned not only with a partner's educational philosophy, but also with personal beliefs:

> I've seen personal beliefs come into play this year, not just professional beliefs, but personal ones. If you don't agree with them, they can get in the way. If I don't like the way this person thinks, her prejudices can get in the way. Those beliefs will creep into your teaching in what you say or don't say. It will come out.

Others mentioned that they would look for partners who complemented them. When we interviewed Pearl, her partner was in the room, preparing for the next day. When Pearl stated, "Each of us has separate strengths," her partner chimed in, "I see that as a challenge. Pearl is good with crafts, and I like to think of projects. A lot of times, she'll know how to make it work. She's taken art classes, and that helps with the expertise. And Pearl helps me spell." After a few giggles, Pearl continued, "My partner is good about positioning things. I'm [leading the class and] talking about things, and I may have visuals turned sideways so they aren't seen properly." Her partner concluded, "So we help each other."

Hillary wrote in her journal about days when fresh ideas eluded both partners. "To be completely honest, each of us has 'one of those days' about once a week." Helping each other was critical under these circumstances.

An ideal partner is versatile enough to cope with the unexpected situations that continually plague teachers. Hillary gave this example:

> On various occasions, one of us will get wrapped up in conversation with a parent, another teacher, the principal, the nurse, or the counselor. It seems as if we're always trying to contact or locate somebody for one reason or another. When you get them, you'd better communicate then, or it just gets put off. The other teacher will begin the les-

> son or activity until the partner returns. At an appropriate time, we will relay the information and clue each other in.

To uncover a prospective team partner's philosophy, Lynne would do several things:

> First, I would think about people I know: who they are, how they teach, and what they're like, probably someone who came out of the University of Nevada about the same time I did and who would be on a similar wavelength. Next, I'd participate in the interview process by using the Professional Development Center's inventory that deals with rank-ordered issues. Then, I'd observe them in their classrooms and ask them whether they used or were familiar with particular programs like Math Their Way and Come With Me Science.

While there is no one common philosophical similarity identifiable to successful teams, the pervading notion of a "common view of the child" in a classroom dominated the teachers' ideas on how to find a compatible partner.

Classroom Climate

A second major area, classroom environment, also dominated responses on finding ideal partners. Some teachers focused on the importance of creating a positive, productive atmosphere; others were concerned with noise levels, neatness, and discipline.

Jill and her partner aspired to create a classroom where students, teachers, and others would want to spend time, a place where kids would feel safe and inspired, as evidenced by a great deal of student writing. Jill would look at a prospective partner's room to see if she felt happy and comfortable in it and if their standards of cleanliness were similar. Beth put it more directly. "I could not stand a total slob."

Summer echoed some of these ideas. She, too, would like to visit the prospective partner's classroom in order to observe the teacher-student interaction, listen to how the teacher talked to and with children, evaluate the teacher's expectations of the children, and determine whether the classroom seemed too structured or too lax. She would try to decide whether the purpose of the classroom decorations were adult-centered or were used to stimulate student thinking. As Lee Anne put it, "You can pick up a lot of things by seeing teachers with their kids—not just in the classroom, but other times, like computer time, music time, or just walking them down the hall."

Denise wanted to give prospective partners the same opportunity. "I'd want to see them in action, and I'd want them to see me in action, too."

While most partners did not make a value judgment on correct classroom climate, they emphasized that different climates needed to be able to coexist.

Discipline

A third key issue in selecting a teammate was classroom discipline. Phyllis said, "I'd look to a commitment—for manners and discipline in the classroom and high values." If she was given the opportunity to question a prospective partner, she would ask, "How do you want your children to behave in the classroom?" and "What would you do to achieve that?"

Showing her concern for children, Helen would wonder of her prospective partner, "Is screaming at students OK in the classroom?" Pearl added the following wish list:

> I'd want a person who isn't afraid to discipline. I'm not a person who likes chaotic behavior. If a person was too lenient, that would bother me. You don't have to be exactly the same, but I think you have to see discipline in somewhat the same way. Be consistent and follow up on rules.

Although flexible about curriculum issues, Claire was not as willing to compromise her discipline strategies. For example, too much noise—even constructive noise—drives her to distraction. This year her partner, Gayle, who was more tolerant of student noise, accepted her partner's need for a quieter classroom.

Another team teacher, Clara, revealed, "I want someone who sees children as children and not as little robots who will sit [at] their desks all day long. Students need to get up and have some freedom, have some choices in what happens in the classroom." Bea said she wanted the teacher to have empathy for students, but at the same time help them to grow and change—"a steel rod in a velvet glove."

Personality Traits

There seemed to be a common set of personality attributes that the teachers in our study looked for when selecting a teammate.

Flexibility was a major concern. Pearl said, "I'd want a fairly flexible person, a person who is not afraid to try new things." Clara responded, "My partner should be somebody who will be somewhat spontaneous and doesn't get upset if we don't follow exactly what's in the lesson plan." Sharon summed up flexibility this way:

> Flexibility is a whole range of stuff. If we start something and it's just going dead, we look at each other and say, "It's not working." Then we go on to something else. When some people have changes in their schedules, they freak out. My partner and I just go with the flow.

A positive attitude was another necessary trait for many of the respondents. Claire wanted someone who was upbeat and animated. She definitely would not want a "deadpan" who would make her feel like a "goof." Pearl spoke for her partner and herself when she said, "Neither of us can stand negativity. I think when you're working with children, it's devastating if you're negative."

"There is something you sense when you walk into a classroom," Summer added. "You can feel if there is a positiveness about the class; you can sense that children and teachers want to be there learning." Sonia added, "Without positive self-esteem, communication will break down." Dale offered an example:

> Last week my partner and I were feeling rushed, and we found that we were both feeding each other's negativity on kids, on life, on school, on where we were going, on "let's hurry up and get this school year over with." That hadn't happened to us generally over the previous years. Each day I found myself being more negative, and she was, too. We were feeding each other and causing it to compound. We have to watch for that. We have to help each other.

She suggested a solution. "Say to your partner, I know you're having a bad time, but I'm sure feeling bad, too, and I think we're hurting the kids. Our attitude needs a little adjustment here."

A third attribute, a sense of humor, was mentioned several times as an important trait. Renee said, "I'd want someone who likes to play in the classroom. Learning has to be fun." Toni suggested laughing together, while Jody recommended asking a potential teammate, "Do you consider yourself a humorous person?"

The attribute of trust is not only the most difficult to find in a teammate, but also seems the most difficult to develop in a partnership. Helen was adamant about the importance of trust. "I would absolutely have to trust that person," she said. "I would switch grades before I would team with someone I didn't trust." Irene pointed out that trust developed from working daily with a partner and seeing what the other did. However, Margaret stressed, "We come to any relationship with our own baggage, and that affects our dialogue in the relationship."

Sonia believed that issues of control and trust were common with beginning teams, but said that in her team the problem lasted only four months. "As soon as we both felt comfortable with the knowledge that each team member knew her stuff, we relinquished the control factor." She also thought that the second year together was very different from the first year. "The partners don't have to work out issues of trust and communication, and they are free to be both humane and fair to one another without losing their sense of self." These teachers felt lucky that their principal made it very clear to them in the beginning that they should remember at all times that they were equals. Jody concluded that team teaching can make both participants feel secure in their teaching.

Another trait some teachers sought in a teammate was personal compatibility. Gayle, wanting to be friends with her partner, might ask, "What would you like to do on Friday afternoon when we're finished teaching?" Similarly, Gladys revealed that she and her partner had "supportive personalities." She explained, "We want everything to be OK and we take charge of that. We are both mothering, that kind of personality."

An additional component for a potential teammate is the willingness to grow. Phyllis noted, "I'd want someone who wanted to learn—learn from the children, learn new methods of teaching, and be willing to try new things." Barbara added, "True professionals are those who are willing to grow."

For Joan, a compassionate and nurturing manner is a necessary factor. She said that while "realizing that everyone has cross moments," she felt that "kindness must be exhibited at all times." Melanie said that if she is irritated by something that happens during the day but ignores it, in a few days the irritation disappears because it will have been replaced by something positive her teammate has said or done. But Sharon said, "We believe that we have to let the other person know how we are feeling and what we're thinking, what we like and don't like, and we're very respectful of our individual differences."

Several team teachers focused on the need for a sense of equality and sharing. Sally warned that no one can completely own anything in a team classroom. And Margaret emphasized:

> I wouldn't want somebody who had to be the chief. I'd want someone who would balance my strengths. I love teaching reading, but I wouldn't want to be someone who said, "I love reading; it's my strength, so I'm going to do it all."

Gayle maintained that teachers have to let go of their own egos to appreciate the strengths and positive aspects of their partners. Margaret shared the following:

> Since I was doing remedial group work with students in a sectioned-off portion of the room, I felt isolated and felt I wasn't bonding with the kids the way I wanted to. I said several times to my partner, "I don't want to be your aide." Finally, one night after work we went to [a restaurant], and I burst into tears. She said that she felt what I was doing was the most important because if those little ones can't learn to read, they're sunk. So we changed some stuff around and took turns doing the opening things, and then I found myself feeling ridiculous. They cared as much about me as they did her, and I decided to just let it go because I was getting behind and not able to get that first reading group going fast enough. So I told her, "I've changed my mind. Let's go back and do it the other way again." We try hard when discussing problems to say "I feel" instead of "You're doing."

Commitment was also emphasized by teachers in the study. Kelsey wanted her partner to have the same dedication to the job as she had. She stressed, "It can't be someone who comes at nine and leaves at three and is down in the lounge every recess." Two other teachers had similar views on this issue. Sharon reported, "My partner and I come out on weekends. On three-day weekends, we usually spend one of the three days either at her house or at school." Adele felt that a partner needs to be willing to spend time outside school getting the program set up. Mavis worried that if the team members were not balanced in their time commitment, the students would recognize it and perceive it as a weakness.

Another important consideration was a potential teammate's interaction with students. One teacher suggested observing the partner from a student's point of view. Sara proposed putting herself in a student's place, asking, "Would I like this person to be my teacher?" Joan thought that the rapport between student and teacher was paramount. She would ask, "Do children seem to trust the person and go to [him or her] freely?" Phyllis would just listen to the language that teachers used while talking about children, asking herself such questions as "Did they seem tired of the job? Did they seem to like children?"

The ability to tolerate differences also seemed critical to successful teaming. Dale shared details about a team at her school:

> We never expected them to be successful because they were very, very different from each other. One is very religious; the other is a smoker, likes to go out and dance, is athletic, and pats you on the back. It's amazing how well they have done. I think the bottom line is that they respect each other. Each could say, "I would never have done that, but it sure did work!" Teammates must respect one another—which I think has to do with the way that they think about a child and the way that they approach their job.

The division of labor has not been an issue with Susie and me. We agreed when we first started working together three years ago that there were things that she would do because she had no children of her own. Since we are close friends, there has always been an understanding of the other's needs.

When we write our lesson plans, we make a list of preparations for the week. This list is put aside for parent volunteers. Most of the time they are able to complete 90 percent of the prep work. If it doesn't get done, we discuss the issue (usually the day before it's needed). Then we volunteer for the job according to what we can fit into our lives. Since I have two little girls, Susie often has stayed after school to complete what's necessary. I take additional work home so I can be with my family.

This year Susie has a new baby so the scenario has changed somewhat. She has let me know she won't be staying long hours. This is fine with me. I take work home, and volunteers do the rest. It is necessary that I understand Susie's needs—just as she has understood mine for the last three years. Our team teaching is not a competition; rather it's something we work at together. Because neither of us is a robot, the division of duties is something that occurs according to each of our needs.

Since both of us are in this profession to teach, neither one of us is content to sit back and be an aide. (At one point in our first year we tried that!) So our routine includes doing a whole language unit together, then breaking into reading groups. We often read a big book together, or take parts in a smaller book that we read to the class. Then we ask a brainstorming question, give think time, then chart the kids' responses. This works great with a team! While one has her back to the class writing a response, the other is repeating the answer or fishing for more responses.

Since our class is taught in integrated thematic units, we include social studies and science during our whole language time. That way, the afternoons are left free for math, art, P.E., and music. We generally do a whole-group lesson for math, then break into smaller groups depending on the abilities of the students. We have fallen into a routine as far as bookkeeping. In the morning I take attendance and she does lunch count. As far as recording grades, whoever has an extra minute does it. We usually correct our own small group's work. We have a box for papers that need to be copied. Either a parent does this, or one of us checks it and does what's necessary.

This division of labor works for us. I don't think one of us ever thinks the other has done too much or too little. I believe we both feel lucky to be working together. I often think how lucky I am to have such a great partner. The burden is considerably less than when I taught alone! And I think our success is due to our discussions beforehand, as well as our friendship and our understanding of each other.

Candy Humasti
First-Grade Teacher

CHAPTER 3

When the Door Closes: Getting Started

Once the partnerships began, all the worries and what-ifs were put aside as the realities of team teaching overwhelmed the possibilities. After getting through the initial turmoil of solving the whos and whats and wheres, teams faced the big question of how the teams would work. Some team members had the foresight to resolve issues before the need arose. Others felt overwhelmed with immediate, pressing concerns.

Defining Roles

Once the teams were established, the partners had to decide on several critical issues, some concrete, some oblique at best. Because they approached their teaching tasks differently, team members first needed to agree on what jobs were most important. Some felt that planning long-range objectives was paramount. Others felt that getting the room arranged was the first priority. The important point here is that without talking about them, priorities can be the first stumbling block to the relationship.

Most teams had enough time at the outset to discuss all aspects of day-to-day operations. Some established criteria for dealing with issues and concerns, while some left them unresolved.

Talking about division of labor, Lindsay said:

> I think having that couple of weeks before school began to sit down and really formulate a plan for the year, have our discipline plans set, and have a good outline of what our teaching strategies were helped to ensure we were consistent. At times we could split groups when we didn't agree on things. We could still come together for whole-group activities on things we did agree on. I think being together before school started allowed for that.

Teachers needed to decide on specific roles. Who would call the students to order? Who would manage secretarial matters such as collecting notes and money, taking roll and lunch count, doing book orders, preparing progress reports? Who would talk to parents or students needing immediate attention? Who would conduct the whole-group activities of calendar, pledge, and other morning routines? Who would see that the room was cleaned up after projects?

One thing most agreed upon was that with two in the room, one could do the paperwork and the other could start the students on their way, saving a lot of time and frustration. The days began more smoothly, more quietly, and more happily. It was the same with those emergencies that always seem to happen at the wrong time if you are the lone teacher in a room. In a team, problems are more easily handled.

Middle school core teams had a different problem because of the number of people involved. When one person forgot something, it affected other teachers and lots of students. As Liz remembered, "When the pizza didn't arrive, we had to turn a hundred kids away. It was embarrassing for all of us." Core teams also had additional responsibilities—such things as grades, binders, folders, and homework all had to be handled the same way. The more people in a team, the more time it took to coordinate all the details.

Team members needed to discuss the specific roles of each teacher during each part of the day. Because Sonia and her partner both loved to lead whole-class activities, they agreed to share that work equally. When one was leading a discussion, the other might interrupt to share ideas. Because they had agreed to this at the outset, interruptions were not perceived negatively. Rather, both teachers saw them as vital parts of their working relationship.

Leslie asked herself, "I wonder what my teammate thinks I should be doing?" When probed further, she talked about herself as a strong, dominant personality, a person who felt comfortable both planning and leading classroom activities. She was not sure she always wanted the dominant role, but she was also not sure she would be comfortable being passive.

Some teachers agreed to divide the lead teaching according to subject matter. Gayle, the more experienced teacher, chose to plan and lead the reading–language arts block while her partner planned and led the math lesson. During whole-class instruction, Claire moved around the room supporting individual children, while Gayle led the reading lesson. Later, during small-group instruction, each led a group.

As time went on, the division of responsibilities began to be more routine and thus less time-consuming, as this team member commented after two years with her partner: "We both participate in keeping things in order and in doing the management work. This is the first year ever I haven't spent large amounts of time at school on weekends." Managing parties, plays, and all sorts of large-group productions was made easier by having two or more teachers to work with the students. Journal after journal recounted hectic days in which nothing seemed to go as planned. All teachers have these kinds of days, but team teachers seemed to have it a little easier, as one recorded in her journal after one exceptionally disastrous day: "Thank God for teammates!"

Philosophies and Values

While some teachers saw concrete tasks as more manageable initially, others disagreed. They felt they were unable to deal with issues of attendance or even room arrangement until they had discussed other, more important issues: What do we value most in education? What evidence will we collect of student learning? How do we respond to the different learning styles of our students and to our own differences in teaching style? What are the specific outside demands of the teaching partners—children, spouses, other jobs, advanced education?

Sometimes teachers had to defend their teaching methods and curricular choices. If a partner did not approve of a much-loved story, project, or technique, they needed to negotiate. When the effort to negotiate seemed too great, the attempted curriculum was aborted. Some felt it was better to retreat than to put the team relationship in jeopardy. Team teaching is risky business, according to Phyllis:

> We both try not to hurt one another's feelings and would opt to stand off a bit rather than cause friction. We decided that two dominant personalities would not work well unless each was willing to listen and give a little. We discussed several teachers who we knew had dominant personalities, and we agreed we could not team with them.

Mavis and her teammate were both concerned with being seen as dominant personalities in the classroom. Other teachers worried about losing their individuality in a teaming situation. First-year teachers in particular wanted to be seen as viable teachers in their own right, not extensions of more experienced teachers or, worse, teacher aides. Cathryn was concerned about evaluation. When her principal evaluated her partner, Cathryn realized that she altered her own normal teaching role:

> Melissa and I aren't particularly threatened by evaluation observations, so when she mentioned that she had decided to invite our principal to observe during a science lesson that she had planned, I had very little reaction.
>
> At the appointed time, the principal arrived, and normalcy departed! As the principal settled in, I looked at him and said, "What's my role here?" He shrugged his shoulders and laughed, "I'd hoped you'd have that figured out." My question was half joking and half very serious. I realized that he would need to see my partner "perform" and that I would need to be cautious of my participation so that I would not interfere with the lesson sequence. I also felt that I could not become a mere observer and risk leaving Melissa without support and leaving him with the impression that our teaching style was "sequential." I felt terribly uncertain of what I should be doing. Melissa began

the lesson by making masterful connections between what was familiar to the students and what they were to learn. I found myself attending much more closely than usual to how well she was teaching and silently applauded the lesson. It would have delighted Madeline Hunter.

We came to the part in the lesson where class participation and some writing began. As Melissa completed her instructions to the students, I began to circulate to the students who I knew would need some assistance. Each time I leaned over to speak to a student, Melissa was beside me. I moved away to check the progress of others and found Melissa beside or ahead of me each time. It did not take long to realize that I was actually making her uncomfortable. I backed away.

During the rest of the evaluation period I tried to appear to participate in the lesson without actually doing anything. The normally free and informal dialogue between teachers, which serves to reinforce important ideas, became inappropriate because of the need to adhere to a more formal lesson sequence. The usual support offered to children became uncomfortable because of the need to "prove" management abilities. Our normally easygoing exchange of responsibilities and support became foggy, and neither of us was very certain of our roles.

Later, pondering the evaluation session and its outcomes, I began to think about what I see my partner do each day and tried to isolate the specific strengths I see in her teaching. I realized that my principal had witnessed and recorded a "perfect" lesson, but had missed the whole story. He had not seen my partner skillfully elevate each child's self-worth by praising a response or redirecting wayward attention by including a child in discussion. He had missed an entire array of skills that show an expert teacher in action. I felt cheated. Because of the structure of the evaluation process, he had not been able to truly appreciate the masterful teacher I watch each day.

The following morning, Melissa and I spent some time sharing impressions of the session. We laughed about being disoriented by the observation and agreed that we were not terribly satisfied by the way it had gone. The good news is that we both had confidence in the fact that this one session meant very little to our administrator and that Melissa felt perfectly at home sharing our "role confusion" with him as they discussed the evaluation session.

Discipline: Sharing the Responsibility

Elementary teachers beginning to team teach frequently raised the question of whether discipline could be handled consistently with two adults in the room. It is interesting, however, that discipline—even in most of the dysfunctional teams—seemed to take a back seat to other problems once the team got under way. It may be that with two adults in the room, the students were just better behaved, but it seemed to the teachers that two different personalities in the room allowed them to handle small problems before they became big ones. Jill stated:

> Well, B. was back today. At the the beginning of the year, he did not bother me as much as he does now. Joy and I seem to have taken a turnaround with him. He really bugged her at the beginning of the year but doesn't now. I'm not sure when or how this turn took place. It's good one of us can handle him in a positive manner.

Classes with special children, like the one above, benefited from having two adults in the room. These classes suffered much less disruption, and the special students often made better progress because of individual attention. Pearl described one particularly memorable child:

> This child had been expelled from three schools. I mean we're talking about someone who's seven years old. We had all of this prior knowledge before he came, but we just decided we weren't going to have any preconceived notions about him. But he lived up to his reputation, believe me! He came into the classroom totally disruptive and ornery. We just double-teamed him, quite literally. Eventually he was so good. The teacher of the learning disabled had been working with him and the counselor. He had friends. He was starting to read and was doing a super job with math. We felt good about him. Then the court moved him. As luck would have it, he was going into another team situation. We talked to one of the team teachers. He sounded very caring. Last week they called up and said everything was great. We felt so good, we were ready to cry. If I'd had him in a single-teacher classroom, I'd have been climbing the walls.

Teams found modeling learning behavior for the children easier with two adults present. Acceptable social behavior was also demonstrated casually, because the teamed adults usually treated each other with mutual respect, something some children were seeing for the first time. The teams also modeled simple ways of resolving differences with young children.

Dealing with Insecurities

A substantial number of teachers expressed concern about looking incompetent in front of another professional. They felt that alone they could relax and enjoy teaching children, but worried about doing so with another teacher present. Would they make silly mistakes from nervousness? Would their teammates do the same? Would their teammates be forgiving?

According to Phyllis, "My new partner has felt a bit strange and not really settled because we are thinking together rather than on our own." Several teachers reported worrying about failing as team teachers. Clara thought that if she and her partner failed, the other faculty members would think less of her. Sonia and Violet, on the other hand, felt enormous pressure to succeed because they saw themselves as test cases for their entire community. If they failed, team teaching would never be tolerated again in their school.

Space and "Stuff"

For many teachers, addressing the more concrete tasks of teaching proved critical. How would the teachers decide on the arrangement of the available space—student space, teacher space, and storage space? Where did the teachers' desks belong? Did they want student desks or tables? Where would activity centers be most effective? What materials would be stored in the classroom? How would bulletin boards be maintained? Would the classroom library contain teacher-owned books or library books or both? Would it be better to move both teachers to a new room? If there was no choice in the matter, what must the teacher currently occupying the room do to welcome the new teacher? When is it acceptable to take children out of the classroom for portions of lessons or for individual attention?

According to Sonia, "The greatest problem we have faced is storage. There is simply not enough room for all of our things." She reported that her first major blowup with her teammate was because she neglected to follow through with her commitment to provide storage space. Being the new teammate, her partner chose to stay quiet about her lack of space until one day both teachers forgot an important ingredient for their project. Sonia's partner said heatedly that if she had a place to store some of her things, she would have been able to provide some of the supplies they both needed for their work.

Virginia discussed logistic and monetary problems. "Things I could do with a small group became a madhouse with thirty-two. Plus, thirty-two of everything is more expensive if your partner doesn't want to put out the money."

The issue of neatness came up several times. Pearl said:

> I think teaching style has a lot to do with success. You can have someone who is a total neatness freak or someone who is not as organized. My partner is wonderfully organized, and I love her for it. My desk is never quite as neat. If someone was too sloppy, that could be a problem. We always pick up after a project; neither one of us likes glue on desks and great globs of paint.

Sharing Personal Materials

Children's books are expensive, and others might not take the same care of them as their owner. When teachers buy things for the classroom using shared money (PTA allotments, grants, or book points), who owns the materials if the team dissolves? If one teacher wants to do a favorite project that requires personal spending, should the partners share the cost of the project equally? If one teacher is more financially stable than her partner, should she bear more of the costs of the classroom expenses? Tiffany spoke of division of labor and materials:

> My partner and I bought materials for the classroom separately, but we used them together. When we purchased things together for the kids, we gave them to the kids, so there's nothing really to divide. We came in with our own books and our own bulletin boards and our own materials, and I've bought more throughout the year because I didn't have that many, but we really didn't buy anything together. And we filled out separate lists of what we want in the classroom next year, because we think that whatever is purchased for the teacher stays with the teacher, not the classroom. I know it would be hard for me to choose what was going to be used in this classroom when I had no plan on being here.

Time and Schedules

"There is not enough planning time in the school day for team teachers. Productive teams manage to plan, but they always pay some kind of price," said Barbara, a "push-in" team teacher. Not only did she need to see a great many students in a variety of settings, but she needed to plan with each of their classroom teachers.

Other teachers were also concerned with time management and planning. When teaching alone, they simply planned the lesson and taught it. Now they had to plan the lesson, agree on that plan, decide which teacher would take which role during the lesson, and agree on a method of assessing both the lesson and their teaching practices. This much planning seemed burdensome and frightening to many, particularly in the first days of the partnerships.

For elementary teams, the clock seemed to be their biggest enemy when it came to planning. Pearl commented:

> I think planning is one of the major problems in team teaching—trying to get enough time for the two of us to plan our activities. Some whole-group activities we plan together; then [for] our small-group activities, we just plan what we're doing with our group as an offshoot of the whole group. You just have to trust what the other one is doing. We communicate with each other to make sure that we are covering what we need to cover. We do planning together, and we do separate planning. It has to work that way because of the time factor.

Many elementary teams tried to use the music or P.E. period to plan, but their journals reflected that other things often interfered. Planning usually ended up being done after school. One middle school team had "Sacred Thursdays." Neither team member made plans after school on Thursdays so they could plan the next week.

In her first interview, Joyce said, "No matter how long it takes, we put down on the plan sheet exactly what we're going to do and who's going to do what each period. We have a little symbol for each of us that we put in a little box next to each activity that makes it really clear who's going to do what." This team had chosen to teach together and knew ahead of time that all planning would have to happen after school.

Some high school teams had common prep periods, but some did not, depending on how the schedule at their school was arranged. One of the middle school core teams had a common prep, but the other did not. The need for more time to plan and be truly ready to teach was a common thread that ran through all the interviews and journals.

The planning process, however, was a joy for many teams. When asked if teaming helped her be innovative, Liz responded:

> One hundred percent! It's astounding! It's amazing! I had taught seven years in the traditional way. I knew what the English curriculum was. It was locked in my head. In February, I liked to do poetry and activities about Martin Luther King. I had it set out by the month. When I started teaming, from September on everything was new. I don't want to sound negative. You can reuse a lesson, but do you always have to teach it on September 4? I find teaming so exciting. We've come up with some exciting things that I would never have thought of—absolutely never. It is not only innovative—I can't express how innovative—but exciting. You run to the research room because you want to. We have this astounding two-week unit that would take one person hours to plan. But I just did my part and the others did theirs.

Merging Two Minds

The importance of flexibility—the ability to merge two minds into one plan—was also mentioned in many interviews and journals. In the following conversation, Pearl and her partner Martha discussed how they handle differences:

> *P:* Well, I think we take the tack that if either of us is that opposed to something, maybe we'd better take a good look at it. It is probably not going to be that successful unless you can find some common ground. I don't think we've ever had anything that we've been that far apart on.
>
> *M:* It's funny, because about the time when I think I can't stand the way something is going, my partner will come back and say, "You know, I think we should do it this way." I'm ready to go along.
>
> *P:* It also seems that with two people, you know even sooner if something isn't working.
>
> *M:* Yes, it's amazing how things will go along and then we'll both look at each other and say, "This is not working! What are we going to do?" So

we change all of the time, from room arrangements to the way we group.

P: We don't think we have the perfect plan and we may never get to that point. Usually when we've changed, it has been for the better. We're making progress.

Some Last Words

> My partner and I looked at each other the first day, and thought, "It's not going to work"...the day from hell idea. We knew we were never going to survive. Then, one of the students ran out of the room. I took out after him while she continued the lesson, and I thought, "Maybe this teaming *can* work."

While there seems to be no magical formula for success in team teaching, a commitment to making it work seems to be essential. As Eldris explained, "I was committed to making it work for the preservation of our friendship, for the assurance of our professional integrity, and especially for the sake of our students." That professional dedication seems to underlie all successful education. Each teacher must discover his or her own formula. What works for one doesn't necessarily work for anyone else, and the magic simply is not there every minute. Whether you are a solo teacher or a team teacher, the magic is in the moment—especially since change is the only constant in education.

We are screaming at each other so hard that our faces are contorted with the effort to produce more sound. Her mouth is open wide, and she is leaning toward me. I cannot hear what she is saying but I can clearly see her anger. The dream is vivid and so horrible that I am shaken when I am finally awake. Questions and uncertainties push sleep away, and nighttime fears of failure become so real that I cannot imagine that I can have actually agreed to this nonsense. Daylight brings exhausted calm as I have convinced myself once again that not only can I survive, but actually flourish, in my new role as "team partner."

Cathryn Williams
First-Grade Teacher

CHAPTER

4

Changing, Growing, Becoming

As Angela put it, "There's a lot involved in team teaching that people don't know about, or even think about, unless they've encountered it," and that first encounter carries with it apprehensions, hopes, and expectations that surely color its outcomes. Whether they became a team by choice or to satisfy some outside need, participants reported that once the decision to team teach was final, emotions vacillated between energetic excitement and night-sweating terror.

Entering the Team

Beth put into words a feeling common to many: "It's really a very, very scary thing." Most teachers wanted and expected team teaching to be a good experience for them and their students, but they also had some reservations about day-to-day functions. Worries and fears centered around losing control within the classroom, losing spontaneity and flexibility within the day, and infringing on a partner's territory (or, conversely, being infringed on). Self-doubts plagued teachers: Will I be a good team player? Am I good enough to teach with my friend, Mrs. X, whom I respect so much? Can we get along together every single day? Will I still be able to teach the way I love to teach and teach the things I love to teach? Even teachers who very much wanted to be part of a team had initial doubts and fears.

However, along with these reservations, many spoke of the excitement they felt at this new challenge and the high hopes they held for the possibilities now available to them. Teachers were eager to work closely with an equal partner, sharing ideas and techniques, combining strengths, dividing tasks, collaborating, and discovering together how best to meet the needs of a diverse set of learners. New and inviting avenues to professionalism lay open to them.

Our participants described "teamness" as comprising many elements: mutual respect, trust, confidence in the other person, and a deepening sensitivity to how this other person might think and feel. This team unity, which seemed essential to successful teams, was not always present in the initial stages but was greatly strengthened after teams had spent time together engaged with students.

At first our teams devoted much time and energy to the process of creating a team—a new and separate educational entity. When a new team was created, our participants found themselves stepping back in order to move ahead, confronting issues as a team that many had already resolved within their individual classrooms. Veteran teachers found themselves establishing new routines for management and organization, borne of the need to combine two established styles into a single system. Novice teachers began the arduous task of creating systems that represented the best ideas of each team member. In both cases, the process of compromise was time-consuming and required a great deal of communication.

Becoming Comfortable

By working together to establish classroom systems, the teachers began to gain some insight into their partners' needs. Many in our study reported that as this first year of team teaching began, partners were very cautious about these needs and were concerned that nothing upset the delicate bond being formed. Communication was tentative, and concern for the other person's feelings was central in verbal exchanges. Some described this time as a "honeymoon" period during which the partners "walked on eggs" to keep stress out of the classroom. Later, many felt less need to tiptoe and became more direct and open when communicating about classroom matters. Eventually, many found a comfort zone in which each was able to assert some individuality without infringing upon the other.

When asked exactly how this comfortable partnership evolved, several related simply that mutual respect and trust grew over time. Only by actually working together in a classroom for a time could they create a bond strengthened by common commitment and history. Irene stated, "The bond between us has grown. From a shaky beginning, a strong foundation has been built."

A growing personal friendship contributed to the connections between successful team members. The intensity of that friendship ranged from the partners' spending a great deal of time together outside school to their seeing each other only at school. Many participants spoke of caring and the sharing of everyday lives as ways to enrich the team relationship. Julia said that "sharing life events" had provided the groundwork for her and her partner to understand their students' lives better.

Growing Respect

Growing trust between partners helped teachers let go of many classroom issues. For example, planning, which at first ate ravenously into the time teams spent together, gradually began to take less time. In the beginning, teams sharing instructional tasks needed to talk through every element of each lesson, together choosing an objective, lesson sequence, method of presentation, and the part each member would play.

Later, many of these same people could communicate much more briefly about a lesson. Less needed to be said about lesson details as partners began to recognize and have confidence in each other's strengths and abilities. These teams were able to share instructional tasks. Each partner could move into and out of the leadership role according to what seemed most appropriate to the situation. They became fairly certain how a partner might react to a particular idea and began to feel free to move away from the more rigid schedules with which they'd begun.

Once such rapport between partners had developed, more flexibility within the day became possible. Spontaneity crept back into the classroom. Planning together became a time to share ideas about curriculum, content, objectives, and methods of presentation rather than a time to assign tasks.

Communication

Some teachers reported that the need for time with their partner was eased when they took courses together. Class hours provided additional discussion time, and course content provided a shared knowledge base from which to discuss issues specific to their own classroom. Several reported that these courses helped resolve issues that might never have been resolved otherwise. The teachers spoke of the excitement of trying new ideas together and developing activities that grew out of ideas presented in the courses they took.

As the school year progressed, some partner teachers found that a system of nonverbal communication emerged. At least one team made a specific effort to devise such a system, but for others, this communication developed unconsciously. It seemed to be more a product of the team's growing familiarity. One partner began to sense what the other was likely to think or feel, and body signals such as a shrug, a glance, or a nod confirmed the message. Decisions and changes could be made without interrupting the flow of the lesson. These teachers were able to recapture and capitalize on the teachable moment.

The process was not easy and the way not always clear, but during their first year, many of our teams evolved into units of strength to which each member freely contributed his or her own unique talents and style. Members of these successful teams were quick to recognize both the difficult challenges as well as the many advantages of becoming a team. Teams were a new way of teaching, and the partners had to evolve into it. They had to learn to think of team teaching as giving each partner equal opportunity for input.

Beyond the First Year

Those teachers who were together for a second or third year spoke of requiring less and less out-of-class time together. Sonia said that comfort came from "having done it and feeling successful last year. The change and the flow that occur over the year make the difference." Second-year team teachers mentioned gaining confidence in their ability to make certain decisions for their team independently. Several mentioned fewer discussions about the division of labor within the team and more detailed discussions of curriculum and methods.

For most, the second and following years of team teaching offered more rewards and fewer frustrations than the initial year. Sonia reported that during that second year, partners could "read each other's minds, know where you're headed, and know how you're going to get there. If something happens, the other can keep on going toward that space."

Unfortunately, not all teams reported the success just described. Many were never able to reach a point where partners were comfortable within the team. For some, the sense of "teamness" never emerged. "Team derailment," according to our participants, happened for a wide variety of reasons. Some had personal or philosophical differences. Others mentioned too much "togetherness." For some, communication broke down. And some realized that a team required "team players" and that they or their partners were simply not team players. Yet, in spite of a difficult team situation, some of these teachers said that they would like to try team teaching again with a different partner.

Team Teaching Means Transforming

Whether a team described itself as successful or unsuccessful overall, the relationship between the team members and the nature of the team partnership were dynamic and ever changing. Being part of a team affected the members who composed it. The individual members, in turn, constantly affected the nature of the team as they attempted to meet both their own and their students' needs.

A never-ending evolutionary process seemed to be at work for the teachers participating in our study. For most, in spite of the hard work it required, team teaching was seen as positive. The satisfaction gained from meeting the challenges offered by team teaching seemed to enhance the self-confidence of the participants, and whether or not they intended to continue the team relationship, many felt pride in having come so far together.

Teachers cannot help themselves: they change and grow and change again. For most, this evolution proceeds as teachers work in their own rather isolated classrooms, taking from each teaching encounter whatever they are able. Team teaching, with all its baggage, decreases isolation and increases interaction with at least one other person. Time and again, participants related stories of personal and professional growth that they attributed to the experiences available to them while working in a team. The following passages from participants' journals express the enormity of change and growth they experienced:

> Teaming has taught me many things. I've learned how to be more patient, more flexible, to accept ideas and criticism without taking it to heart (well, sometimes). It's taught me commitment, dependence, independence, and partnership. I've done a lot of growing this year. Because I team, I have become a better listener. Teaming has forced me to do that. My team partner and I cannot literally talk to the students at the same time so when she's leading a lesson, I'm only there to support our "community," our classroom. In the beginning, I had to force

> myself to zip my lips at times so that I wasn't interrupting. This was not an easy task, but I feel better about myself having improved in this way. *Hillary*

> As the year progressed, I became more comfortable teaching with Sonia. She treated me with respect. It never seemed to enter her mind that I was less able than she. She never questioned my ability. Trust developed, and I knew if I made a mistake, I wouldn't die of shame. In fact, I think once I saw Sonia make a mistake. *Michelle*

> Every year is a growth year for me, but this year I gained a lot of confidence knowing what teaming is about and knowing that I can work that closely and well with someone else. She's learned from me; I've learned from her. *Irene*

Partners Learning from Partners

Along with their statements about growth in overall confidence and ability, some of our participants were more specific about particular kinds of valuable information that they had gained from working with a partner:

- Sara found that "I am enjoying this learning experience as far as how to organize centers—management-type things."
- LeeAnne saw that "sometimes I think Kelsey observes [the children] better than I do. It makes me more aware, and then I try to watch the next time and follow up on it."
- Denise, after watching her partner in relationships with students as well as adults, learned that "everyone has something that makes them special and unique."
- Claire picked up on her partner's positive responses to students.
- Sharon was excited to have a partner who was a recent college graduate and who would therefore be able to provide practical information about whole language teaching and literature-based instruction.
- Because Lynne appreciated the way her partner conducted parent conferences, she observed at first while her partner led them. Later, their discussions about conferences helped Lynne gain confidence and take the lead during some of the conferences.

Generally our participants seemed to value this rare opportunity to observe and learn from another practitioner. Teachers could watch as their partner worked with a particular technique and could explore approaches that might enhance their own teaching style. Seeing new ideas presented in familiar day-to-day settings made the ideas truly useful.

For many of our participants, recognition of this professional growth was a pleasant outcome of the team teaching experience. Jody even suggested that team teaching is a good inservice technique: "I learned some team building techniques while watching my partner do new lessons from her classroom management training. This is such a good way to learn and see new ideas from workshops or conferences."

Helping Each Other

Some team partners had common goals for professional growth. For example, one team focused on creating a developmental classroom in which expectations and activities were geared to meet the needs of the child at his or her current level of maturity. Working together helped the partners maintain their focus; they could remind each other of the appropriateness of an activity for a particular child and examine and adjust tasks based on their separate observations. They commented that they had the luxury of an ever-available coach to evaluate and celebrate progress toward their shared goal.

Taking Risks

A number of participants mentioned the value of having a sounding board for testing new and perhaps risky ideas before implementing them in the classroom. These teachers felt encouraged to take the risks in their teaching that might enhance their effectiveness. Sharon's comment is typical: "Having another person to help plan and implement opens doors to try things I wouldn't attempt on my own." For the most part, teachers felt supported and encouraged to take risks, and they often witnessed their own growth as a result of the experience.

Becoming More Creative

Some of the team teachers mentioned that the positive reinforcement they got from their partners gave them greater confidence in themselves and that, as their confidence grew, they would try more creative activities. In addition, with two people contributing to the creative process, teaching became more innovative. Putting two heads together produced a richer, more varied idea pool from which to draw. Within the safe environment of the team, members were more willing to blaze new trails. Dale liked having someone say, "Yeah, that's great. Let's do it!" She also enjoyed having someone to talk with after the lesson. For her, team teaching provided the impetus to stretch professionally and then, later, the means to assess the outcome. Team members who were able to attain the trust that promoted this level of exchange discovered powerful tools for instructional improvement. Many perceived their team experience as a fertile time for professional growth and improvement.

Analyzing Teaching Experiences

Of course lessons failed from time to time, but reactions to these failures were generally positive. Teachers spoke of not being afraid to fall on their face because a teammate was there to help pick up the pieces.

Some teachers, however, were not as positive about learning through failure; they were somewhat embarrassed to have been observed when a lesson had not gone well. The private upsets that are part of every teaching career suddenly became more public. Overall, however, our participants maintained a sense of humor about their mistakes.

Whether discussing success or failure, team teachers spoke of the value of feedback from an invested equal and of the growth they experienced as a result of that feedback. While most successful teachers do a great deal of self-evaluation, team teachers found themselves verbalizing and explaining that evaluation. Talking together while planning, structuring, and assessing activities allowed partners to discuss the pros and cons of particular teaching techniques. As teachers talked together about how well techniques worked or did not work, they discovered the elements of instruction that produced the most successful outcomes. The information gleaned from these conversations was translated directly into improved instructional experiences. Many felt that the team experience had promoted accelerated professional growth by validating and strengthening the positive elements of each teacher's style while encouraging still greater improvement.

Meeting Students' Needs

In some cases, teachers' relationships with students changed because of team teaching. Kelsey and LeeAnne noticed that having two adults in the room increased the energy of their teaching and that their students found this stressful. They began to adjust the pace of activities so that students could experience greater success and feel less pressure. Shared observation and continual monitoring allowed them to pinpoint this problem and adjust instruction to meet the needs of their students.

One teacher reflected in her journal that she'd been able to postpone identifying a child as a special education student and reach an alternative decision:

> We do not agree about one of our students this year. My partner sees him as special education and I see him as "developmentally delayed." After testing we are still at the same point. He has no learning disabilities at this time, and we are still in the same corners. By doing a possible retention, we are at least able to agree on how to work with him. Probably we are both right. He's not ready for first grade, and later some learning disabilities will show up.

In another case, a child who would have been dismissed as a discipline problem by a single teacher was more adequately assessed through shared observations:

> Sharing the duty of disciplining Matthew…really helped us maintain our sanity and reward Matthew positively. After discussing what seemed to work and sharing hopeful ideas, we set up a special curriculum for Matthew. This was much easier to plan, not to mention

> implement, as a team. Matthew was able to complete his modified assignments, creating even more positive feelings. It would probably have been very easy on my own as an overworked teacher in an overcrowded classroom to write Matthew off as a discipline problem. But as partners sharing and discussing Matthew's tiring habits, we were able to give him a challenging but positive first-grade year.

Maryanne taught at a middle school where the new core team concept was adopted schoolwide. One of the advantages of this core team teaching was the ability of one group of teachers to work with one group of students. This allowed them not only to integrate curriculum but also to instruct the students in skills (such as conflict resolution, for example) that might help them become better students. The power of these student/teacher team dynamics led to the evolution of peer counselors; the student counselors were a natural outgrowth of the core team teachers' commitment to teaching students to assume the responsibility of handling their own problems. Maryanne wrote:

> We feel this is a natural occurrence if students are given permission to solve their own problems and teachers give up some control. We found that most students, if taught the proper techniques, can help other students talk to one another to solve problems. We, the team teachers, do not send discipline problems to the office, for two very important reasons. One, we have very few classroom discipline problems, because the individual members of the student team (and the student team as a whole) will not tolerate a member who causes problems in the classroom—team self-esteem is very high. Two, when a problem arises between student team members, student conflict facilitators are given the task of helping the members peacefully resolve their conflict. Of course, adult team members are always available to help in sticky situations, but very seldom do we need to intercede.

Another teacher reported that she enjoyed watching the thoughtful and considerate way her partner related to students and that she began to pick up some of these techniques. Another saw the value of using "I messages" with students and began to use them herself to deal with problems. Several mentioned feeling more patient with students in the presence of a teammate. Many times, team partners mentioned that when dealing with difficult students, it was helpful to be able to have another teacher step in and defuse the situation. That way, everyone could calm down, and all became winners. Roseann related in her journal:

> Noise, if it's useful noise, does not affect me adversely. My partner finds it hard to take, so we had to sit down and really discuss this. We had to figure out a system that worked for the both of us, with rules and consequences acceptable to both that we could enforce consistently. We did not want the children to be confused. We did not want two different sets of rules for our classroom.

Above all else, concern for the children seemed to be paramount with all the teams. Gloria, a high school teacher, told us how her team handled difficult students:

> Students that maybe I didn't get along with, she could. Or else if there was a student neither of us got along with, we could bring some humor to it and relate to each other's frustrations. That seemed to relieve the pressure and, consequently, we began to relax with the situation, which was good for us and good for the student.

Bea, a member of a high school team that combined special education and freshman English, explained how they handled what she described as the "jack-in-the-box syndrome":

> Stuff one kid in his/her seat and two others pop out of theirs. June's class had three LD [learning disabled] and two EH [emotionally handicapped] students. One of the EH students was already a legend for classroom disruption. June and I decided to try combining them anyway; after all, we could always go back to separate rooms. If you'd walk into that class now, you'd marvel at how well behaved the kids are and how well they stay on task. My partner says the same kids are still awful in other classes with her. It's not that either one of us works magic, but something happens when we work together. She says things I don't and vice versa. We give moral support, and we've had to learn to be tougher than we want, though now we can relax. We still keep wary eyes on what's going on, but it's working. And it takes away guilt. Alone, I think, "Maybe I am just picking on so-and-so." When both of us perceive a problem with the same kid, I quit doubting.

A growing amount of research links the absence of caring adults and good role models with poor outcomes for the increasing numbers of at-risk children. Children from dysfunctional, single-parent, or two-working-parent families have few opportunities to observe and interact positively with adults going about their lives. Team teaching broadens children's experiential base in new and exciting ways. A second adult in the classroom offers greater possibilities for children to observe, model, and develop positive communication skills and well-rounded attitudes about adult relationships at home and at work. They have more adult examples, sooner, with which to compare their own ideas and thus come to some ownership of their own beliefs. As one high school student put it, "Having two teachers' opinions helps you learn to make your own opinion."

After our teacher-researchers had synthesized the data they had collected and thought about what students in team teaching situations experienced, they identified eleven possible benefits team teaching offers students:

1. Another adult to go to for emotional help without waiting in line. Children like the support and immediate attention of another adult.

2. A wider context in which children can stay tuned. With two teachers speaking and moving around the classroom, children do not get lost or fall between the cracks as easily.
3. Translations. One teacher translates for the other, giving students a second (or third or fourth) voice and perspective.
4. Options other than special education for the child who cannot follow the typical routine of the classroom and needs some extra help to keep up.
5. Opportunities for more individual instruction and interaction.
6. Diverse personalities. Two or more teachers mean more talk, more to listen to, more fun.
7. Opportunities to get organized and to get going more efficiently, to get to the real learning at hand.
8. Opportunities to play one teacher off the other. If one says no, a student can ask the other. They can negotiate.
9. Opportunities for students to broaden their notion of who can be a teacher.
10. Models for collaboration that students can apply to their own work in groups.
11. Better assessment and evaluation of students (especially in "push-in" situations) because expectations of students are more fluid when they are based on two people's perspectives.

Working with Parents

All teachers know that there are two kinds of parents: the ones seen and the ones not seen. As a child progresses through the public school system, teachers find more of the latter and fewer of the former. However, nothing seems to bring parents to school faster than their discovering that their child is being exposed to a pedagogical technique they did not experience during their own schooling. The familiar is safe and comforting; the new tends to be threatening.

This phenomenon was especially true at a middle school where the whole school started core team teaming. This bit of advice for helping parents adjust to new systems came from Maryanne, a core team member:

> This year we've really reached out. We've gotten parents involved. We have team parents. We had an ice cream social in the fall. It was an educational night for the parents. We did some real short interdisciplinary units with them—about five minutes. We moved the parents around from class to class just like the kids move. Then we had a basic session at the end where we asked them about complaints. It was the way we should have started out our first year. I would recommend to anyone starting out on something new like this to do such a program. It's like inservicing your parents.

The elementary team teachers usually contacted parents by note or had a parent meeting at the beginning of the year to explain team teaching. Most teams found parents very cooperative and willing to work with them as a team. They usually did not tell parents which students were on each teacher's list. The teams tried to get the parents to understand that all the students had two teachers and that both teachers were going to work with the students together. They also made it clear that report cards would be done with the input of both teachers. The united front seemed to make even some of the teams who were having problems feel more comfortable when working with parents.

Becoming a Reflective Practitioner

Time and again, in many different ways, our team teachers emphasized the reflective nature of a team—and the power that reflection gave them. Team partners shared their observations of students, their relationships with students, their lesson plans and evaluations, and their teaching methods and styles. These exchanges allowed each member of the team to talk with a completely invested equal about educational issues in a direct and meaningful way. This dialogue helped (and sometimes forced) many to define their own educational philosophy and clarify their own beliefs. For many, such thoughtful reflection brought new empowerment both personally and professionally.

Many of our participants recognized and valued this power. As Faye put it, "I think I'm a better teacher with someone else in the room. I think I'm more aware of what I'm doing and why I'm doing it." And Phyllis summed up: "Teaming is so powerful. It's the most powerful teaching I've ever done."

One of my journal entries was about the depression I felt after losing my partner. Teaching World Cultures (World History and English combined in a two-hour block) was Denise's and my baby from its inception. When we finally got the approval to do it—the time in the school day, the description in the school handbook, and the fifty-six guinea pigs—we went for it. Coming back periodically in the summertime to map out the school year and to develop lesson plans became stimulating and fun. Basically, we mixed and matched the literature and English to fit the units in World History that I had already taught. We had a blast developing, scheming, creating, and enjoying each other's company. We had had no direction nor advice on what worked, how to organize two hours, how to divide our time, or how to set up the classroom. We never thought about discussing our personal philosophies, attendance, discipline and consequences, or personal effort, and it didn't seem to matter either because we just naturally fit together—like Cinderella's foot and slipper. Things just evolved.

That was September through January. One cold, windy, snowy, miserable day when we both had colds, morale was low, and exams were approaching, Denise told me that she had applied for and been hired by the district personnel office. A condition she asked for and was granted was to be able to finish out her teaching year—because of our program. I cried and whined and felt betrayed and depressed for weeks. I had it all figured out that we would spend the next summer revising, revamping, and creating anew and, of course, enjoying each other and having fun with it.

And yet the year was still special even with the knowledge of losing my partner hanging over my head. We experienced field trips, talent shows, taking kids to the opera, end-of-year parties, so many special things, that it was hard to let go. But Denise left, and I had to start again.

Ginny Young
High School Social Studies Teacher

CHAPTER 5

Endings

Ironically, one of the first concerns of beginning team partners was how the team would cease to be one. Yet some teams never addressed the issue of dissolution, probably because a team-teaching relationship begins so tenuously.

At a summer training session, a number of new team members expressed their concern about remaining friends with their new team partners when the team dissolved. In our study, team teachers seemed to give friendship a high priority within their working relationship. Shannon revealed, "At the beginning, my partner and I agreed, 'If something happens and you don't want to team anymore, you have to tell me. If you really hate teaming, you must let me know.'" Margaret's partner also displayed foresight: "Actually, my team partner asked me before we started, 'If I left you in three years, would you be OK?'"

Whys

Inevitably, and for a variety of reasons—retirements, promotions, staff reallocations, student redistributions, funding decisions, personal dissatisfaction—teams broke up. Whatever the reason, there never seemed to be a smooth adjustment. Even unhappy partners regretted being a part of a team that was terminating.

Violet echoed the feelings of many teachers when she said, "I'd be upset. It would be like a divorce." Sonia also likened it to a divorce, adding, "What an emotional death! Like a part of your body was no longer attached." Claire agreed, saying, "My partner knows what I need, and I can tell when she needs me as well. I'd feel lost if my partner weren't there."

Some of our participants suggested having the school district provide workshops to deal with the emotional aspect of dissolving a team. Others suggested that individuals take on that task. Even when the reasons a team dissolves are not threatening to individual self-esteem, there are still emotional issues that can be left unresolved.

Beth was concerned with adjusting to teaching by herself again. "Since I've been a member of two successful teams, I'm thinking, How am I going to deal with all this by myself? I've gotten used to teaming. We know what we are doing. It's really tough to get back into thinking how to handle it on your own."

Retirements and Promotions

The reasons for dissolving a team that partners found easiest to accept were retirements and promotions. Phyllis elaborated:

> My teammate is retiring, and I've known since we started. Because we know that, we started talking about little subtle things. She is lamenting and struggling with the fact that maybe she doesn't want to retire.
>
> We would truly love to have one more year to get more cooking together. Probably between the two of us we've each said that about three times during the year. It's our way of saying, "I'm going to miss you; there's more I have to learn." Also, I've found myself most recently being very complimentary to her. It's my way of letting her know, "Being without you is going to be tough." Just thinking about our team's ending almost makes me cry right now, and I haven't cried about it yet.

Reallocations

Several of our respondents' teams were terminated when one or both members were transferred to another school. Some said they were unaffected by these reallocations; others became depressed, angry, and resentful.

"If we were told because of numbers, classrooms, or whatever, we were going to have to split up, we would not be happy about it. We would still remain really close friends, though. But if we were told that that was the way it had to be, then we would just accept it," Sharon predicted.

Others reacted differently. When Bea learned that she was being tranferred, she coped with her team's termination by avoidance. Even after her partner's new partner had been designated, she still felt somewhat possessive of the team and the class. She struggled against it by helping that team plan for the following year.

Beth's partner was also forced out because of staff reallocations:

> My team is ending because my partner has the least seniority at our school. I will have to teach by myself next year, and I'm really enjoying my team. If more students enroll next fall, then she has until September 20 to come back. We have already discussed that possibility and made the principal aware that we would like to reteam in that event. I am not ending this situation happily.

Then Beth focused on helping her partner find a new position. "Having been in the district longer, I can help her with contacts and things she needs to know that will help her. Sometimes I offer suggestions; other times I just wait for her to ask." Beth suggested to team partners who face this same situation to be open, let the leaving partner talk about it, be willing to listen, and be sympathetic.

Twyla's team ended when decreasing enrollment forced the two to draw straws to determine which partner would remain at the school:

> It came down to being very personal, even though it's a professional relationship. My team partner and I had to figure out which one of us had to leave. The only fair way to do that was to draw names. So at that moment, it split up the team, dissolved it instantly. We had a wonderful year. It's sad to see it end this way. It's sad. I feel sad. And I don't know how she's feeling because she's stopped sharing everything. She's fine professionally, but I don't know what's going on behind that.

Twyla went on to say, "I don't know how to do this right." She did suggest, however, that the district amend its reallocation policy to provide for and acknowledge the profound accomplishments of a successful team:

> Shouldn't there be special provisions that allow teams to stay together in this situation? If the teams are successful, then shouldn't the goal be to keep them together? In our case, because of numbers, rules of seniority, and such, we're getting split up. There is no special help for us to go together somewhere else or to stay together here.

Personal Dissatisfaction

Endings were most difficult when one or both teammates were unhappy with team teaching or with each other. Some found it impossible to accept each other as equals and to share responsibilities, power, and students equally. Sometimes team members had problems because team teaching drained them of energy; some simply needed a change. Eileen offered, "It would be easiest if we both just felt our team wasn't the best for the kids and the best for us. I think if you have to think about that type of thing, it's probably best to end it." Lindsay said:

> I am really uncomfortable talking about this. It's been awful, and I'm sure my partner said the same thing. We've just had some situations where it is so childish; it's been ridiculous. I'm just trying to make peace for myself. I've said, OK, I've got five days left; I'll be as pleasant as I can. But I'm not going to be her best friend when I'm not feeling that way about her. I don't want to act like, Oh, I'm so happy to see you, when I'm not. I'll be friendly. I'll work. We've had a lot of meetings that I've had to deal with, and I've been there for that. But that's it. That's where it stops. I'm just trying to be civil. If I am at this school next year, we still need to be able to communicate and have that cooperation. I have definitely learned a lot; it was a learning experience.

When teams were in the process of dissolving, insecurities surfaced. Leslie questioned:

> How will my partner react? What does she think? Will our team's ending reflect on our teaching abilities? What did we do wrong? Were our expectations too high? Too low? Do we have nonteaming, noncommunicative personalities? How will our ending affect others? Will oth-

> ers be required to team, to fill our places? I don't like the idea of forcing teaming. That can backfire if the teachers are only "salaried employees" and not true educators thinking first of their students.

Some teachers dreaded losing face with valued peers. As Clara explained, "It's happening to me now. I think on both of our parts, ending will be kind of a relief—not necessarily that the team is over, but it didn't work out as well as we had hoped it would. People are always assuming that something happened between us, and that's not the case."

Dale and Pearl also wondered what other staff members would think. "Now if one of us were not wanting to teach with the other one and wanted to establish a new team, I don't know," Dale said. "That would be sticky." Pearl added, "If she came to me and said, 'I want to team with Stacy next year,' I could understand it, but it would hurt my feelings."

Amy speculated that dissolving teams could cause other teachers to become apprehensive about team teaching. She suggested that when dealing with curious staff members on the subject of a team split, one should try to be honest without divulging too much. Nevertheless, team dissolutions often affected other teachers in the school. Virginia noted:

> It doesn't seem fair that a teacher who can't get along with others gets "rewarded" by being allowed to teach alone. We have a bitter split-up at our school. While it wouldn't be a problem for us to end a team, it is a problem for the team at our school who didn't get along. I had thought it would be easier to end an unsuccessful team than a successful one, but I guess that's not true.

No matter the reason for a team's splitting up, both members risked being exposed as "weaker" or "lesser" teachers. Worrying about what other teachers on the faculty think added to the pressure.

How to Get Out

Once team members knew they would dissolve their partnerships, they were often concerned with avoiding hurt feelings, dividing materials, moving on, and generally just easing the transition.

Avoiding Hurt Feelings

"You don't win friends and influence people if you let your partner overhear your unhappy feelings or learn of them through workplace gossip," Leslie warned. "Always talk with whoever needs to know; and if you're planning to end a team, talk with the partner first—unless you have a very good reason."

Because her team was splitting up at the time, Angela was uncomfortable discussing the subject. Part of her discomfort centered on how she had learned about it—through gossip. She felt that a partnership should be dissolved in a professional manner and that there should be no hard feelings carried into the next year. She offered words she might say to her partner: "We both tried hard this year. Something went wrong that we can't fix. Maybe next year, we'll have a better year apart."

According to Dale, the issue of hurt feelings would not be a problem when her team split up. "We both would prefer to be by ourselves. Since we know that about each other, there should be no hard feelings." She readily admitted, however, that circumstances would be different if only one member of the team wanted to end the partnership. Clara commented on that situation:

> It would depend on the relationship with your team partner. It's happening to me now—our breaking up. I think we're still going to be friends, and we're still going to see each other and do things together. In a way, I think it'll be better for our friendship. The times we'll be together would strictly be to have fun. In our situation, I don't think the ending of the team will be very traumatic. It'll just be over.

Martha added, "If dismantling the team is your idea, you have to decide how you want the relationship to continue. If you want to preserve a friendship, you need to talk to the person about why you're quitting." She felt it was important for the person to stand up for him- or herself and deal specifically with the problem. "You have to decide what you need to do for your own self-esteem."

Summer expressed her hope that a team breakup could be handled in a positive way. She felt that even though the relationship might not continue professionally, it could continue personally, and that partners need to be honest and up front. Hillary added, "I try to talk with my partner. I'm getting even easier about it as we get closer to the end of school, a good thing. I think that both of us would say we've had a really successful teaming situation and year."

Margaret wanted her partner to "write something special for me to keep, instead of just sitting down with me and saying how she felt about the year or how she felt about me or whatever. After we did that, then we could sit down and talk about what went really well for us and what didn't."

Dividing Materials

Some teams, realizing that change is inevitable, began their teaching year by planning what to do with materials when their partnerships were dissolved. Shannon and her partner gave this example:

> We decided who'd get which stuff. We did that all year. I don't think we'd fight over anything. Yet if there was something, we would talk about it. If there's something she wants more than I do, then she can have it. I'm not possessive with materials, but we have accumulated a lot of stuff this year.

Sharon and her partner have also thought through the ending phase of their partnership. "In center activities and other things that we've made up, we just agreed that when the time comes for us to go our separate ways, we'll each take a copy of everything."

Hillary and her partner had a unique twist to dividing materials:

> On the stuff that we bought together, we decided what things she could probably use more for second grade and I should keep for first grade. The stuff that is sort of in the middle, we're just going to put out on the desk after the kids are gone and bid for it: I'll take this if you'll take this, or I'll let you have this if you'll let me take this. And, since she'll probably be right next door next year, I'll know what she has that I can borrow, and vice versa.

On the other hand, Renée and her partner did not plan ahead:

> Right now, I'm having a problem and a bit of nostalgia because a lot of our materials have blended. I'm not sure what's mine and what's hers, like independent reading books and bookshelves. I don't know how many I brought in. I'm just trusting her judgment.

Eldris added yet another aspect to be considered when dividing materials:

> Teachers need to realize that while materials can be duplicated, the energy and work going into creating and presenting those materials cannot be duplicated when they become singleton teachers. They need to be aware that if they attempt to do everything by themselves that they were able to accomplish as a team, they will quite probably burn out from frustration and stress.

Moving On

"There is no graceful way to end a team unless one or both are moving on." This sentiment, expressed by Rhea, was echoed by a number of participants in our study. Faye offered the following recent experience:

> I did it by explaining to my partner several months ago that I've always wanted to teach another grade. Then, a few weeks later, I told her I was going to apply for an open position at our school. I tried not to talk a lot about it. She was real quiet about it, and until she knew for sure what was happening to her, there wasn't much communication. Since she knows, it has opened up more, and we can start dividing stuff, what I'm taking and what will stay with her. Now it's real open and sharing. Since we both built the units we have, we both want to keep copies.

Rhea seemed to regret how she treated her partner while opting out of a partnership. She recalled what she had told her partner:

> "I'm going to an upper grade. I don't like teaming. It's not you, I just want to move up." Then I vacillated a while. One week I'd say, "I'm going to try to go to fifth grade," and the next week I'd say, "Oh, let's stay together." It wasn't fair to her.

She believes that her team failed because of the lack of communication. "As it is, the ending was ugly because too much was left unsaid at the end. It's important to be able to talk to the person, even if it is the end."

Monica and her partner were both going to change grade levels in order to make what she termed "a better teaming arrangement":

> We are both moving grades next year so as not to team. We will still do things together with our classes. We are getting together over the summer to plan because we'll both be working with the same grade level. We're trying to get our principal to keep us in the same wing so we can departmentalize. We will still each have our own classroom of kids, but we will have another person to gather ideas from and work together with and team with—basically just teaming in a better way, we think.

Marilyn and her partner plan to reunite under similar circumstances:

> Now that the decision has been made, my partner and I both feel excited and a little relieved. We've already talked about doing our slide show and our field trips together next year. But we won't do as many things together. We won't live in each other's pockets. You literally just live together, almost more than you do with your spouse because you're here so much. I think we both feel we have gotten closer to each other; but at times, we've gotten real tired of each other, and that's been hard. But it's been incredible. When I've been a little bit down, she's pulled me up. When she's been down, I've pulled her up, and the class just goes. It functions.

Easing the Transition

Mass endings, such as a rescission of the class-size mandate, could be professionally devastating for some partners. In that case, it would be helpful for teachers to be given methods for adjustment. Julia offered the following suggestions:

> It seems as though the more positive way a team could be ended, the better. Perhaps one element that might be fun, enjoyable, and meaningful would be for the team members to brainstorm the high points of the year. They might want to break the positive aspects into different categories, such as the best sharing times, the craziest days, the most fun activities for the students, the most fun activities for the teachers, the best assignments and field trips, etc. "Things I have enjoyed most about our team" might be another main topic.

Eldris had other ideas for coping with mass endings:

> It might be helpful for administrators to give everyone some time to absorb the impact and consequences of the endings. Perhaps they

> could then organize planning sessions for groups of dissolving teams. There, they could listen to and empathize with one another's reactions and concerns, thereby bringing a sense of closure. Teachers could encourage and assist one another in methods of farewell, particularly if any of them will be leaving the school. They could collect mementos or photos to display in new classrooms, and offer opportunities to get together to share stories and experiences of teaming.

Julia added, "If the team is having some reservation about breaking up and feeling some sadness, setting aside a future date during which to meet or arranging a special activity or get-together before the actual date of parting takes place might be helpful." Toni agreed. She stated that because she had ended many student-teacher relationships, she would end a team much the same way—by not ending the contact. She would continue to share ideas, materials, gripes, and success stories with her former partner by phone, letter, or visits. And Beth, whose team was dissolving, planned to take a summer class with her partner: "We'll keep in touch that way."

Administrative Involvement

Principals seemed to be in the unenviable position of being damned if they did and damned if they didn't intervene during team dissolutions.

When a redistribution of the student population meant a team had to be dissolved, some teachers felt the administrator should notify the team members and organize the split. Virginia said, "I would expect the principal to tell us." Of course, the big question in that case is what each team member's future holds.

While Dirk felt strongly that the administration should not arbitrarily end a team, Gayle believed that ending a team would be much easier if the principal did mandate it. June said that she resented not being told that her partner was being transferred; it led her to believe that no one in the administration really cared about the team. Maryanne added, "If it was absolutely necessary to dissolve it, an outside person should be involved so that it was not construed as a personality thing."

Unfortunately, some administrators were neither aware nor informed that a team was not working until it was too late. As Shannon explained, most partners tried to solve problems between themselves before alerting their principal:

> At first I'd try to talk with her after school to tell her that I thought she was out of line with whatever—perhaps her screaming at the kids, her dominance, her being too negative with the kids. I would ask her, "Have you listened to yourself? Do you know what you're saying to these kids?" I'd end it by going to the principal. That's after I'd given it a shot—due process, you know. But I would make sure that everyone knew that it wasn't working.

Dale added this view:

> I think I have heard of people who ask the principal to intervene, saying, "I don't like to be in this situation, but I don't know how to say it to her, so could you say this for me? Maybe tell her that you want for me to be with someone else, and you want her to be with someone else." If you haven't gotten along and it's obvious to both of you, then maybe you could just talk about it. If one of you has hurt feelings and the other doesn't know about it, I don't know how you'd do that. Maybe the principal could mediate, but that seems deceitful. If I were in that position, I might consider doing that rather than approaching my partner. It's hard to say.

Adversarial relationships between team members were not the only difficult endings in which administrators got involved. One principal related the following story:

> Additional facility space gained by the transfer of a special program allowed our team to [go back to] individual classrooms. I brought this good news to the faculty meeting and expected them to be pleased. To my surprise, they were not. They said, "It's like you're causing us to divorce, and we don't want to." They insisted that if there are teams again, that they be allowed to be the first to team.

This principal walked them through the issue, pointing out the spirit and probable intent of the law: that they should use the available space. However, in the end the teachers determined that the increased space did not deny them the opportunity to team teach and to share their creativity, expertise, and teaching materials.

Endings and Beginnings

Coping with change is common to both beginning and ending a team. However, an ending contains the added condition of a sense of loss. Any change can be difficult, but one that includes loss can be the most disruptive and difficult. That may be why ending a team is a more difficult transition than beginning one.

Ending a team can include a loss of materials or work facilities, a loss of shared responsibilities, a loss of comradeship and, perhaps most important, a loss of a sense of belonging. Eldris expressed that sense of loss:

> I was disappointed when our team ended. I felt as if I had let my teammate down somehow because she didn't want to continue as a team. I knew I would miss her, and I do.
>
> She had always maintained from the onset that she would rather teach alone, and that teaming was unnatural for experienced, veteran teachers. She was often surprised and incredulous when I commented on successful teams.

> In spite of all this, I firmly believe she was a wonderful teammate for me. She was, and is, supportive, hardworking, and an outstanding educator, dedicated to providing her students with the best possible educational experience. Additionally, I am convinced that we were a very successful team. Our students learned and flourished, as did we.
>
> I could not face the mental and emotional task of adjusting to a new teammate immediately after the dissolution of our team. We are both in single classrooms now. I am afraid if we had been forced to remain partners again this school year, it would have resulted in a less than positive experience for us, and thereby probably for our students.
>
> I am glad we are in single classrooms this year; I am grateful for the opportunity to have teamed last year. My only regret is that if I had not teamed, I would not miss her now.

And then there were the difficulties of beginning again, as Adele expressed:

> Ending our team was a real big decision. I mean, for us it was kind of emotional, almost like a marriage. We've been in here together with these kids, pooled all of our resources and materials, and it's going to be harder to end the team than it would be to stay together. We were excited about beginning the team. It was neat. And ending it, all I see is work and starting over again.

A friend of Julia's was ending her team and was convinced no better partner existed than hers. Julia reflected on their situation:

> It was so, so positive, and the two teachers blended so well together that my friend didn't think she could be happy in another teaming situation because it could never be as good. The many, many positive aspects could not be duplicated, so she is considering teaching as a single teacher again.

Julia herself had spent the last five years with her team partner, during which a very trusting relationship had developed:

> We know how much time and energy it took to build the trust, the confidence, the caring. It would be a major decision on either of our parts to enter another teaming experience, even if we knew it might be as positive as this one, because we know how much effort and patience it took. It was a definite investment of time and energy into the program, into the students and their academic/social/emotional growth, and into our relationship.

Phyllis, whose former partner was retiring, talked about orienting a new partner. She said, "It's been a yearlong process, and I think the sooner a team knows it will end, the better the team members can prepare to deal with it. I've tried to prepare the new team member, plus tell her all the nifty things, how fun teaming is." She also said that her replacement team partner deserved a Purple Heart for patience and caring:

> We never took the time to bond. My former partner and I had been special friends before teaming. If I knew then what I know now, I'd have set up the new partnership much differently. Because I was still hurting and wishing that my former partner was still my partner, I failed to allow my new partner equal time to assimilate herself into a new environment. It took us until the second year to revamp, make changes, create new ideas, and restructure some of our programs. But we've done it.

Joyce, a veteran ender-beginner, recounted her experiences with ending a team relationship:

> The first time it was like an anticipated death. I went through a lot of denial, followed by anger and finally acceptance, with fear that I couldn't handle it on my own. Most of the students were devoted to the partner who was leaving and to the team. Because it happened midyear, we had a ceremony with the kids where they read poetry by candlelight. That seemed to help. The second time, I knew my partner was temporary, and it was the end of the year, so it was easier to end. Now I'm in total denial that there's even a hint of having a new partner—number four—next year.

Endings were a time of reflection for many. Clara said, "I think when it comes to the end of the year, we will become more reflective. Actually we started to do that today—talked about how some of the kids were at the beginning of the year, and how they are now—and it seems so long ago."

Barbara said that no matter what happened to her position the next year, she would remain committed to taking with her whatever she had learned. "Since I've gotten over the fear of team teaching," she added, "I would willingly do it again. I'll only grow."

And as Leslie pointed out, ending a team is not all bad. "Teams should not be forever. Growth is so important, and we often have to change in order to grow. The question is, when is it time to change?"

Phyllis and her partner believe that the ideal partnership takes about three years to form. As Phyllis put it:

> We feel that in every new teaching position, three years is the charmer. During the first year you scratch and dig trying to put it together; the second year gets better; and by the third year, you've got it running pretty well. For me, by the fifth year, I need something else to do.

Problems the first year were worked out with lots of tears! Susie was very frustrated after she first moved in because I neglected to clean out the math cupboard. Finally, one day she came in very angry and we had it out. It came to tears for both of us. It was awful! I cleaned out the cabinet and she was happy. It's a mess again, and I know it drives her crazy. Any problem a partner has enters into the mix.

Candy Humasti
First-Grade Teacher

CHAPTER

6 The Downside of Team Teaching

No relationship runs smoothly all of the time. Reading and rereading the comments from team teachers for common themes regarding the downside of team teaching, we came across one recurring phrase: "Teaming is like a marriage." Just as marriage partners have their ups and downs, so do the participants in team teaching relationships.

Accommodation

Sometimes the presence of another adult in a classroom that before had been a teacher's sole domain presents problems. Clara and Renée had been friends for a few years before they chose each other as a teaching team. In one of Clara's first journal entries, she reflected on the things that had changed in her teaching—some for the better, some for the worse:

> I think the one thing that stands out for me is simply the presence of another adult. It took some getting used to. At the beginning I often wondered what was going through my partner's mind. Am I living up to her expectations? Is she judging me?

The principal tended to talk primarily to Renée. Clara felt left out, but she knew that the principal and Renée had worked together for several years, and she finally decided that she was just being overly sensitive. She discussed her feelings with Renée and a few of the other teachers, and eventually the difficulty went away.

As the long days of March approached, some personal differences began to boil up. One of these was Clara's penchant for neatness. Renée had made a few earlier comments about Clara's cleaning up the classroom. One day while Clara was wiping down the student tables, Renée said, "I can't believe you're doing that." Clara thought nothing of it and continued to clean. The next day Renée said, "I talked to a friend of mine about your cleaning the tables like you do. She said she never does anything like that."

This time Clara was mildly offended. Not long afterward a discussion in the teachers' lounge centered on the neatness of another teacher. Renée interjected, "You'd never want to team teach with Clara. She's a little too neat for me."

Clara was embarrassed, not because of her neatness but because her partner had poked fun at her. She wrote it off as Renée's being defensive about her own messiness; but, she realized, "if I had made a derogatory comment about her messiness, she would have definitely been offended!"

As spring approached, the mood became darker. Renée's negativity was beginning to rub off on Clara. Renée had decided to quit team teaching and had nothing good to say about the subject. Clara decided she would like to have a classroom to herself as well but didn't see how that could happen given the current overcrowding in the school. As the year closed, each was discouraged and disillusioned. In a final entry in her journal, Clara stated:

> It's like a marriage gone bad. The year is winding down. I hate to say I'm glad it's over, but I am. It has definitely been a learning experience, to say the least. I can now say I've teamed, but would not even begin to know how to tell somebody what makes a good team. We have had some great times as a team, but I'm not sure if the negatives don't outweigh the positives. I've come to the conclusion that as a fairly new teacher, I still need that time on my own to develop my teaching skills and my curriculum. In comparing last year, when I taught alone, to this year, I'd have to say that I felt better about last year. I felt my kids learned more. I was more creative and more in control. I believe you give up 50 percent of the control, which may or may not bother people. In our case, I feel it bothered both of us.

Classroom Space

Another issue that troubled some teachers was classroom space. When thirty students and two teachers are put into one room, problems arise. For some teams, just setting up the classroom was a real challenge. A few of the teachers tried to run separate classes, dividing their classrooms into equal halves with a drawn line or a jerry-built partition (bed sheets hung on a wire, for example). This often proved ludicrous.

As one teacher stated, "It's difficult for my group to be reading aloud when the math group is jumping up and down while they play a math game just ten feet away! We would like to act out stories, but we're so limited space-wise that it's not possible."

Another teacher shared these thoughts:

> Teaming is very delicate. You have to keep your bounds. Quite frankly, it took me several months to realize that I could be difficult for my

> partner or that my partner could cause me any stress. We were too busy sharing our ideas, knowledge, and becoming adjusted to our children. The aspect of teaming that I was not aware of was the little things. Little things can become big things when not solved.

Communication

Many of the team teachers stated that good communication was central to their success, but added that it is not easy to achieve. Each member of the team must feel secure in his or her own abilities and not become defensive.

Some first-year teams had a difficult time, especially if they were also first-year teachers. Amanda said:

> It's not as easy as I would like it to be, and maybe it's because we're both first-year teachers, and we get real defensive. And it's not that you're criticizing each other, it's just that you both have different ways of going about things. You've gone through all these years of school with this ideal of how you will do all of this [teaching], and all of a sudden you can't do it that way. You can do your portion of it, but then you have to sit back and relinquish control to the other teacher. And you're on pins and needles because it isn't what you want to say, it isn't what you want to do. It's real hard to talk about things with another teacher without sounding like you're criticizing. And you aren't criticizing. It's just that your basic philosophy is the same, but your ways of teaching are different.

When asked about how she felt about team teaching in general, Amanda replied:

> I think it's a good way to go for the children, but personally it is really difficult. There's so much give-and-take all day long it's like being thrown in with a roommate. In college you find a friend with whom you really get along, and you live together. Then you find that you could be better friends if you didn't live together. I sometimes feel that it would have been so nice to have graduated a few years ago in order to have had the opportunity to have my own class just for a while. I think that everyone should have the chance to develop her own approaches.

Amanda concluded that her enthusiasm had been squashed and she didn't want that to happen. She felt it would be very hard to remain excited about teaching if she had to remain in the same situation the following year.

Another first-year teacher, Roseann, felt that she and her partner had started out with the same ideas but found that their methods of teaching drew them further apart. She also wanted a room to herself where she could develop her own style. She wanted to be able to try ideas without feeling she needed to discuss them with a teammate. The feeling of needing to have that first year of autonomy came through clearly in many of the interviews.

Monica came to team teaching reluctantly. Her principal told the staff that three, possibly four, teams would be established in the first grade, and it eventually came down to picking a partner or being placed with somebody. Monica and her partner decided to team not for the love of team teaching but so that they wouldn't be teamed with someone else.

At a focus group meeting after Christmas vacation, Monica was quite verbal about her dissatisfaction with her team situation. She liked her partner but felt the workload was lopsided. An aspect of team teaching she hadn't considered before was that one partner could become the lead teacher while the other became a helper. She admitted that she had not expressed her feelings to her partner, but she was determined to get things settled.

The day of confrontation was a Friday when Monica was late for work, at least ten minutes behind the tardy bell. When she entered the room, all the children were sitting quietly reading their books. Her partner was sitting at her desk looking through her lesson plans.

"Did you tell them to get their books out quietly and read?" asked Monica.

"Yeah, we were waiting for you to take roll."

"Why didn't you do it?" Monica asked incredulously. She had had it by then, but instead of screaming and yelling, she decided to wait until lunch to discuss it.

During that discussion, Monica learned that her partner felt the same way: she was making all the parent phone calls for conferences, monitoring morning seat work, and collecting and stapling papers. She felt she was doing a lot of the busywork while Monica was doing the teaching.

Monica reflected on the situation:

> It was really hard talking to her, and that was not an expectation of mine. I thought that because of the way we spoke last year it was going to be really easy. If we had a problem, I thought we would be able to talk to each other about it. This was something that had been eating away at both of us for a while. She had been feeling the same way.

After the initial confrontation, things seemed to smooth out. Monica and her partner began to divide their duties more evenly:

> Things seem to be going pretty well between us. My partner is now helping with the attendance, calendar, and writing on the chalkboard. We no longer look at one another to see who is going to do the next thing. I feel now that a lot of the tension between us after our confrontation is gone. I believe that our team as a whole is working out OK since we've cleared the air. Things have been very positive. Communication is easier now—not easy—but easier!

However, Monica and her partner finished the year by each agreeing to move to a different grade in order to avoid teaming together.

Irreconcilable Incompatibility

Communication is never more important than when it has completely broken down. Marilyn, a second-year teacher, found herself in a quandary. She was new to her middle school and had been teamed with a more established teacher to teach an English–social studies class. She had high expectations of team teaching and was looking forward to the experience. By February, however, her viewpoint had changed:

> This is one of the things about team teaching with Phyllis that drives me crazy. She has scheduled—and of course, she told me and didn't ask me—a speaker for English/social studies. This guest is speaking for two hours the next three days. Not only do I consider that bombarding the kids, but when I asked her if I could have a few minutes to go over my upcoming assignments, she got all bent out of shape. Then she embarrassed me in front of the kids because I wasn't aware of a schedule change. She condescendingly said to me, "I told you before, the new schedule is on Monday. We've gone over and over this!"

Later Phyllis was away at a conference for three days. When she returned, she did not even acknowledge Marilyn's presence in the room:

> Every so often, Phyllis gives me the cold shoulder. I never know why or when it will happen. She just treats me as if I were invisible. I don't expect to be the first person she seeks out after being gone for three days, but I did expect to be acknowledged when I walked into the classroom. Not so much as a hello, and when class was over, she had nothing to say to me. I thought she'd want to know what went on while she was gone, but she didn't seem to care even when I offered the details. She came to my room later for a few minutes, stood and glared in her condescending manner, and then left! I tried to tell her what we were doing, but she didn't care. I know that on Monday she was probably tired from the flight, but on Friday I tried to talk to her again and there was no difference in her attitude. I was told when I was offered this job that she had an extremely large ego that needed continual stroking, and that some of her bad moods necessitate this stroking, but sometimes I get so sick of it. I feel like I'm dealing with a child, and then I feel childish for buying into it.

Marilyn began to feel guilty about her feelings of dissatisfaction with Phyllis. She was constantly thinking about her situation and the treatment she was receiving from her partner. She felt insecure about her knowledge of the curriculum, a feeling Phyllis reinforced, usually in front of the class. Marilyn hated to acknowledge her insecurity because she feared it would once again be used against her.

In March, two-thirds of the way through the year, Phyllis adjusted the class syllabus. She didn't tell Marilyn about the change ahead of time; she just did it. This prompted Marilyn to apply for a position at another middle school, and the assistant principal of that school arranged to observe Marilyn's teaching. On the day he was coming to class, Marilyn was in a panic. She had planned to discuss a chapter she had assigned the week before; however, only two of the students had read the assignment. Phyllis agreed to help Marilyn out. The big moment arrived, and Phyllis put on a great show. The kids loved it, and the visiting assistant principal appeared to enjoy the class (if Phyllis had been applying for the job, she probably would have gotten it!). Unfortunately, Marilyn interacted with the class only about a third of the time. Phyllis had grabbed center stage, and Marilyn, as usual, was left looking inferior.

At the end of the period, Marilyn didn't know whether to thank Phyllis or slap her. Phyllis had saved the day with her knowledge of the material, but Marilyn could not forgive her for grandstanding, rarely letting her talk, and embarrassing her by pointing out her mispronunciation of an Asian river.

It seemed particularly odd to Marilyn that each time she asked a question, the kids would look back at the visiting assistant principal, then lower their heads. She found out later that Phyllis had primed the kids during the period before, telling them that Marilyn was applying for a transfer. Marilyn now felt like a traitor as well as a failure.

Throughout the year, Phyllis exhibited other behavior that led to the breakdown of this team. She would call on Marilyn, without prior notification, to take the class whenever she needed to do some other job and then would stand in the doorway when she returned, impatiently waiting for Marilyn to turn over the remaining time to her.

Marilyn next decided to apply for a position in another department. She was hoping for support and encouragement from Phyllis, but instead she received condemnation. Phyllis went on and on about how fragile and easily frustrated she was and how Marilyn's applying for another job was the last thing she needed, then informed Marilyn that someone else was interested in teaching the class with her next year if Marilyn wasn't. Phyllis assured Marilyn she was not trying to get rid of her but that she felt perhaps Marilyn was not cut out for team teaching. Marilyn said,

> I couldn't believe my ears. I just thought to myself, "This is the ultimate paradox." I am to the point where I just want to quit. Why try to fight people who deliberately try to undermine me? Although I feel relieved to get this out, I don't feel any better about my current situation!

As the year came to a close, neither Phyllis nor Marilyn saw too much of each other. Marilyn summed it up this way:

> I never even approached my expectations of team teaching. I never got the chance. Maybe I will someday. If not here, then somewhere else.

Planning Time

Teachers pointed out other issues that were potential stumbling blocks in team teaching:

> Time is an important issue, and often those teachers who are successful are strongly committed to giving up personal time. Not all teachers are able to do this. Guilt is always an issue when working with time.
>
> *Barbara*

> Planning has to be done when both of you are in the mood.
>
> *Gayle*

Communicating and negotiating ideas are always difficult, but in the closed world of the classroom such efforts can be either inspiring or heartbreaking. Angela, who felt things were not going well, made this comment in her journal.

> We don't plan together. We need to plan together. One person plans when she has time. I'd rather plan together. I'd like more prep time to plan. Team teaching requires communication. Both partners need to share what they are feeling all the time.

The inability to plan and come up with common objectives and schedules seemed to be a common complaint and an obvious sign that the team was not working. However, finding time to plan together was one of the more common problems for all team teachers, whether the team was successful or not. For Bea and her partner, members of a successful high school team, even a common prep period could not be kept sacred:

> When we first started team teaching, we had a special day of the week when we always met on our prep period. As in any school, it seemed as if there was always some interruption. Sometimes we need to move out where no one can find us—outside of school—because we need a length of time to really work a unit out.

Planning and preparation of materials are always time-consuming for the classroom teacher. With teams, the situation is particularly difficult because two people (or more, in core teams) have to find the time and energy to plan *together*.

Many teachers met with their new partners before the school year began to discuss logistics. Nevertheless, many reported problems during the school year because the two teachers were bringing to the classroom twice the materials, ideas, and preferences they had been used to. Many found that as the year progressed, planning time decreased.

Other factors can affect planning time. Two teachers literally walked the playground together in order to plan weekly activities. One member of the pair was part of a "push-in" program, and they taught together only one hour a day. Since they didn't have any other time when they could see each other, these two teachers had to plan on the playground.

Sometimes principals built a block of time into the day or week for team planning sessions, but this was not common. A few teachers reported that the district's attempt to prepare those who would be team teaching was far from adequate. A one-day workshop was offered, but the teachers felt it did not begin to prepare them for team teaching.

Also, many teams had been formed at the last minute. These teams had no time to consider whether they wanted to get into team teaching or not. In many cases, the two people involved were told on the Friday before school started that they would be team partners.

There's a Stranger in the Room: Substitutes

Needing a substitute is a downside of teaching in general, but it becomes a special issue for team teaching.

When stand-alone teachers must have substitutes, they often view the day and the material covered as lost time. Most team teachers, on the other hand, found that if they had to be away from the classroom, it was much less stressful. The partner would keep the students on track. No special lessons had to be written. The partner knew the classroom routine. However, other issues did arise regarding substitutes in team teaching situations. In many instances, the remaining teacher often chose not to have a substitute, but rather to handle all students on her own. As one put it:

> I've found it easier when my team partner is gone to teach by myself. With one member plus a sub, the kids' reactions are so bizarre. At times they can be downright obnoxious! I have found that unwanted behaviors are less severe without the presence of a substitute, perhaps because the other team partner is not being "replaced," she is only "out for the day."

This practice was questioned by other team teachers, however. The following journal excerpt underscored some of their concerns:

> I've heard two people from different teams express the feeling that they would just as soon not have a substitute teacher if their partner was out. This idea leaves me upset and uneasy.
>
> Is teaming really happening if one part of the team is so easily done without? I feel like the purpose for making teams is so we can teach in ways where children have more teacher contact and interaction. What goals do people have for their team-taught classes that are

> different from single-teacher classes? Are students actually benefiting more?
>
> Both team members' being out presented a completely different problem:
>
> When we returned on Thursday, there were two notes from the substitutes. Needless to say, our students did not control themselves in the manner we had asked. Apparently they did not take well to it, or perhaps too well, however you choose to look at it. We left clear and [simple] lesson plans, and our discipline reward system was left in detail in the Substitutes' Handbook. It didn't appear as if either of the substitutes bothered to glance through it. We are not looking forward to both being out again.

Another problem that came up frequently was a team member's being asked to fill in when another classroom was without a teacher because of illness or absence. Many team teachers felt their principal viewed them as just two bodies in a classroom instead of as a unit with two integral components. When one team member was pulled out, the team and, more important, the students suffered. A few teachers were able to convince their principal of the importance of the team unit, but not all.

Philosophical Differences

Barbara felt very strongly that team teachers should share a common philosophy concerning the children. She wrote, "If teachers have a difference in philosophy, they seem to have to choose between prostituting their own beliefs or feeling trodden upon. Perhaps this is a training issue that could be mitigated."

Another team teacher, Liz, expressed a different point of view:

> My strongest conclusion is that what most people view as a negative from the outside—working with someone who does not share your philosophy—is not a teaming negative. It is a personal negative. Communication is not an easy thing to do and learn. People who refuse to even try to work together—well, that is a personal thing. It has nothing to do with teaming.

In some cases, teachers were able to come to terms with their philosophical and personal differences. Others could not, and did not plan to team teach in the future.

The way we teach in our classroom, both of us are present in the room, teaching and helping. The purpose of team teaching is to give children more attention and enhance their education, not to make it easier for the teacher.

This certainly isn't to say that we come to work ill, or that we don't understand that we each have other things in our life that sometimes take precedence. Team teaching provides a built-in support system; each team member respects each other and is there for each other when needed. I find it extremely difficult when my partner is out. I depend on her thinking and opinions and support and laughter, and it's very hard for a substitute to fill that need.

A team-teaching partnership is much like a mother-father relationship. You respect what each member in the partnership does, because when that person is unable to be there for you and for the family or classroom, it makes it very difficult. You try to remain happy and compatible, so that you can teach and children can learn to the best of your and their ability.

RaeAnn Mathews
First-Grade Teacher

CHAPTER 7

The Upside of Team Teaching

Michael was talking with other first graders at his table in the math center as they worked on their *Ten Beads Tall* books. He confided to the others, "I told my mom I want to come to school on Sunday."

"Me, too," said Drew.

"What if we could stay at school all the time!" exclaimed Megan.

"Yeah!" they answered in chorus.

Sharing the Moment

Student reactions like those above are among the rewards of teaching. In this case, it was especially notable because two adults shared the moment. Their eyes met, and they knew they would remember this shared experience for a long time.

For nearly all the teachers in our study, sharing moments in the classroom was a big positive of team teaching. No matter the type of coteaching or the level at which it was done, the feeling of no longer being isolated was mentioned over and over. Martha stated that team teaching created a "more humane working environment." All teachers, no matter how dedicated to the profession and the students they teach, agreed that there were times when being isolated with "just kids" day after day was "sometimes inhumane."

Most teachers have been accused, at some time or other, of talking too much shop at home and on social occasions. Teams found they needed to discuss their work less often outside school because another adult had already shared the joy of a young person's really reading for the first time or the sorrow of teens losing a classmate in a car accident.

The teams shared special moments outside class as well. Many of the journals mentioned that, after school, quiet times were treasured. Gladys offered these thoughts:

> Whew! I'm glad the play production is over for this year. It really took away from time spent with my partner after school. Those quiet times

> to work together in the room and reflect on the day, help each other, and ask each other's opinions are really an important part of teaming.

For the successful team member, teaching was not lonely anymore.

Effect on the Students

Do students benefit from team teaching? Our experience leads us to believe that, when team teaching works well, children are the true beneficiaries. Team members who felt that teams were a viable way of teaching agreed on these positive effects:

- The student receives more individual attention; there is more time to tune in to individual student needs.
- Children in need of special support can be pulled aside in small groups and helped.
- Students are never left unattended.
- Interaction with students increases.
- A teacher is always on hand to help with a thought or a spelling word, or to explain what is expected in the lesson.
- Someone is always available to walk around and monitor student learning.
- Someone is available to answer questions.
- The curriculum moves on even if one teacher is absent.
- There is a better chance of finding out whether there is a breakdown in communication.
- Thought processes can be modeled.
- There is flexibility in paperwork and assignments.
- Students are given less busywork.
- Students can be helped to look for alternatives.
- There is more time to introduce more detailed information.
- There are more opportunities to read.
- Students learn how to ask questions.
- Students are exposed to more ideas.
- Students can relate to more than one teacher personality.
- Teachers can use different skills in different situations.
- Discipline is easier. The partners have the ability to consult with each other and to plan strategy.
- Students can be assessed informally by one teacher while the other leads the class.
- Grading and evaluation are enhanced because there are two views of the student.
- A student's social, emotional, and curricular needs can be discussed with another person who has an equal understanding of the child.
- Situations that develop without warning can be given immediate attention.
- Students can observe a good working relationship between adults and experience a positive role model for adult interaction.

- There is more flexibility to make phone calls to parents.
- Conferences are easier, and the parents get more than one view of the child.

These benefits for the students were summed up by Leslie, who said, "An environment is created in which kids feel that adults are concerned about them." Team members, in general, reported that having more than one adult focused on the needs of the students enabled the students to feel nurtured. They also said that the work environment was more relaxed and less stressful, that students were able to be more successful, and that both these factors, in turn, improved self-esteem and made for a better society.

Dealing with the Curriculum

Curriculum was a major area chronicled in team members' journals and analyzed in meetings. Many teachers felt the curriculum was greatly enhanced when it was planned and executed by a team.

Teams reported that they had more energy to expend when they developed curriculum. They wrote that the curriculum was vitalized through a variety of materials brought in by team members. Teams felt the teaching was involved less with "taking a book and going through it page by page" and more with hands-on projects and center activities. Teachers also liked the fact that there was someone to share classroom expenses for projects, field trips, and other extras they wanted to provide.

Teachers who enjoyed team teaching said they liked having another professional in the room with them. They liked the input, the extra brain power, and the extra pair of hands to help set up projects. Sonia expressed her happiness about having a partner when she wrote, "It's a lot of work, but it lessens the burden—not just in the physical sense, but in the emotional sense."

We found that teams expressed ideas through great brainstorming sessions that brimmed with energy and creativity. Ideas were brought to fruition because more than one person developed and was responsible for bringing in materials. Projects became bigger and more in depth. Lisa reflected this when she wrote:

> This week we've had Oceans Week at school. While it's such a valuable learning experience, it can also be kind of hectic. Having two of us working on experiments, dissecting, and art projects has helped. We share the workload and keep each other sane.

Gloria said, "When you have two people working these types of projects, it leads to more creative ideas, and it sets up more successful experiences for all kids." Gayle added, "The kids get more variety."

Teachers in teams often reported that the curriculum could be more personalized and wide-ranging for those ready to meet the challenge and still be paced to meet the needs of the slowest-learning child, because the team could brainstorm ways of reaching individual students and plan for different modes of learning. Teachers had access to a greater variety of materials, and they used these materials and their collective knowledge to spark and recharge their units. Beth said:

> You don't use the same old stuff. I've come up with some exciting things that I would never have thought of, absolutely never. For example, we're doing an interdisciplinary unit on zoos. It's fantastic. We've focused on Africa's endangered animals. On my own, I'd never even [have] thought of it, but in a team, I'm good at it!

The statement "Two heads are better than one" appeared frequently in teacher journals. Beth wrote about the positive effects of working with her partner on projects:

> She really got into it and made it a lot easier. We did a lot more cooking, painting, art projects—and a lot more writing. By having two of us in there, it really helped. With one teacher, you couldn't have one group cooking and another group doing this or that unless you contacted a lot of parents.

One team partner, Colton, had great writing skills. The ease with which he took his fifth- and sixth-grade writing students through revision made it seem a piece of cake. He had the students produce incredible revisions. He and his partner learned how to make this a vital part of the curriculum, and together they helped students craft their writing.

Many other teams wrote that, because they were a team, they had time to put more writing into the curriculum. They reported that they could get students individually or in small groups to give them feedback about their writing. A student agreed: "With two teachers, I can go up and have the story edited right away."

Jody said, "If anything, it makes the students more relaxed, more reassured; their questions are answered more quickly, and they are able to do their work in a more successful manner because you are able to direct their thinking on paper, whatever the concept."

Teams also reported that the workload seemed lessened because of the shared interest in the curriculum. It was often mentioned that planning time was scarce; yet, when teams did have the time to plan well, they felt their ideas were more creative. As Shannon said, "We are innovative; we do a lot of hands-on manipulatives and that type of thing. And we probably try more than most people because there are two of us."

The teams in our project gave many examples from all levels of education about how projects could be enhanced. They said they saw the potential for taking more field trips; doing more cooking; writing more newsletters; developing more math and science centers; integrating secondary classes in English, history, special education, and ESL; and encouraging more parent involvement. "There are more ideas, and lessons can be taken farther than anyone dreamed," said Jill.

Team members told us that words of encouragement from partners spurred risk taking. June said that having a teaching partner gave her a feeling of confidence, the feeling that she could try something new. When she suggested a new way to approach something, her partner said, "Why not? Let's try it. This sounds like fun."

The journals were filled with anecdotes about words of praise and encouragement. Teams wrote that they learned new or different ways to work with curriculum, and that they felt like taking on more because there was someone there to help shoulder the planning, give energy to the activity, and share the end result. Gayle said of being a team member, "You get a second opinion: should we do this?"

June wrote that she and her partner developed a career unit that offered many more hands-on and practical experiences for the students. She too said that neither partner would have attempted the approach for the unit by herself. After assigning a term paper that incorporated math, business, and economics, June wrote, "I would have been really scared, feeling, 'I'm going to get caught for teaching math, business, and economics in an English class.'"

Teams reported that they felt curriculum was improved because there was not as much lag time in moving from one subject to another. When one area of the curriculum was finished, a team member could make a smooth transition to another subject. Teams told us that lessons were more focused and that the curriculum was more organized. They also felt that there was more stimulation for the students because the lessons were planned by the team.

Ways of teaching the curriculum were as varied as the teams, and they also changed within the day. There did not appear to be any one way to deliver the curriculum. Some teams chose to teach lessons in concert, each chiming in at various stages. Others spoke of playing off each other in a well-orchestrated way. Sometimes team members contributed spontaneously. Some teams divided both the class and the curriculum. Some teams taught particular subjects all year; others traded off, teaching different subjects by days, weeks, or grading periods. Whatever the arrangement, it worked for the particular team. Members of successful teams tended to be flexible, changing to accommodate the needs of the team.

Those who enjoyed team teaching wrote positively about the benefits it had on the curriculum. In general, they felt that the curriculum had been enhanced by input from more than one person.

In short, the participants' journals and interviews were rich with the positive aspects of working with another person in a team situation. Sharon wrote, "The experience of team teaching is more in every way than I thought it would be. It is fun, challenging, and a learning experience." Summer expressed much the same feeling: "I think I've grown a lot. I've been exposed to more materials and different teaching styles—strategies to help." Kelsey wrote: "I learned so much more about presenting new and different things that weren't my style, but which I could adapt."

Conferences

The benefits of team teaching were particularly clear when it came to parent conferences. Team members felt having another person was especially helpful when dealing with difficult parents and talking about retention. About having a partner, Summer said:

> In conferences it really helps. I make notes before we sit down, things that we as team members want to highlight. If we don't have all of the points, my partner will say something to the parent and it triggers a memory of mine; then I am able to give the parent more information.

Jill noted in her journal:

> Conferences are going fairly well this week. So far only two no-shows. We do our conferences together. I know some team teachers who do theirs separately, but I would be so afraid that I would miss saying something important. With my partner there, if any one of us misses something, the other can jump in.

The teams that did have separate conferences usually exchanged information and opinions about each child before the conference. One team found that separate conferences gave them more time with each parent. However, first-grade teachers frequently mentioned that retention conferences usually went much better when both teachers were there to help parents see their child from two points of view.

Even the high school teams found that two handled parents more easily than one. Mavis recalled an incident in which a parent was angry at her specifically, but her partner was able to take over and explained the incident from a different perspective, defusing the situation.

But team members stressed that the benefits went beyond the time spent with parents. They wrote that after meeting with the parents they would process what happened during the conferences. They discussed points that were made and points they would follow up on with the students. Teams felt that the processing they did led to new ways of interacting with the students. Margaret wrote:

> I think the end result is better because your partner is a listener at times and can refocus what's being said and can really make a point if need be. It also makes a difficult conference easier, since two professionals are seeing the same type of behaviors.

Support

Personal highlights for team members who enjoyed team teaching were many. They enjoyed the support received from another professional; they enjoyed the friendships they established; they felt that conferences and relationships with parents were less stressful; they felt that sharing new materials and techniques was beneficial; and they felt that planning sessions were more fun, a time when new and more plentiful ideas could be brainstormed. The teams also said that dividing and sharing the workload made for a better working arrangement for everyone.

The benefit of having the support of another professional in the classroom cannot be overemphasized. Comments about support were written over and over again in the journals. "Classroom teachers often feel quite isolated from one another and set apart in their own niche," wrote Sara, "and that feeling disappears when one is a member of a team." She continued:

> One of the best of these discoveries is the joy of sharing the positive happenings with another. I don't have to tell the story or set up the background of each incident because we have that common information already about events and occurrences within our classroom and school. When a student begins to really read for the first time, when a student joyously shares his writing with others, we can simply look at one another and know that our pride is double.

Of course, this is not to imply that there were not rough waters to be crossed and kinks to be worked out. Team teaching needs to be fine-tuned, kneaded gently, reexamined daily, moment to moment. Team members often referred to the need for constant communication in order to make the team work. "In our team we discuss everything, all day, every day, as much as possible, as often as possible. It gets us in tune with our class. That's what teaming is about," wrote Sally.

It is through supporting each other that a team begins to work. Lynne commented, "We're so lucky, we are so much in synch with each other." Teachers who have team taught know that being in synch takes a lot of patience and willingness to practice. It takes understanding and, perhaps, overlooking those "little comments" or moments of frustration that make one want to throw up one's hands in despair. It is this fine-tuning that makes it worthwhile, because if a team is in concert and is given time to grow, it can work beautifully.

The feeling of not being alone was one of the biggest positive effects of team teaching. This feeling was even shared by many of the teachers in struggling teams and was one reason they would be willing to try team teaching again with a different partner. As one former team teacher said, "I'm so lonesome. I just loved team teaching. Now I just feel so isolated." Another participant concluded:

> If I could no longer team or if collaborating with a group of teachers became impossible, I'd quit. It would be like having to take a giant step backward. I'm too professional for that. I'd have to find another profession.

Sharing the Workload

Team members wrote that it was wonderful to share the workload. Grading papers and evaluating students was easier with a partner. Planning sessions were fun as one idea spun into another. Jill said, "The joy of two minds is endless."

In actual fact, the workload is not lighter, but team members felt that the time spent planning was balanced by a shared responsibility. Jill continued:

> One thing I love about having another person in the room is the ideas that can be generated together. I believe that our units are more creative because there are two of us working on them. With my partner here, we constantly analyze and look back, and if something is not working, we move on.

The benefit of sharing responsibility for big events such as room parties, field trips, and major projects in science, art, and writers' workshop was mentioned frequently in the journals. Many team members reported that they took on more projects as a result of being a team, or they breathed new life into old projects. Some said they could just plain "face the mess" knowing they would not have to clean it up alone. They said that there was extra energy in the classroom and an extra pair of hands available at all times:

> The Valentine party was successful for all concerned. The children had a wonderful time. The parents had fun, and I am not so worn out. It pays to have parent volunteers and a partner to help plan and work during parties.

One of the team members in our research group supported the team concept in a singular way when she said, "Next year, my son will be in first grade, and I want him to be in a team situation, not a single-teacher classroom."

Friendship

Friendship is a cornerstone of life. We need and enjoy the connectedness that comes from being cared for and loved by another human being. Teams wrote profusely and with passion about the bonds that were established in the team-taught classroom. It was clear that the friendships went beyond the classroom.

LeeAnn commented, "Mutual support and admiration on a daily basis, even if it is unspoken, is there—and sometimes that's all I need." Gayle added, "My partner and I are becoming closer and closer, not only as friends, but as colleagues who respect and appreciate each other. I look forward to seeing her each day, making decisions about the day, and sharing ideas and thoughts."

Teacher journals were filled with stories about friendships. Julia wrote poignantly about how close these personal relationships become:

> When I look back upon what our personal lives have held the past four and a half years we have taught together, there are many little occurrences, the ups and downs of everyday living. Then, of course, there are the bigger, perhaps more profound, happenings of life, such as my partner's wedding, the birth of her first child, and the loss we

> both experienced when our fathers passed away. All of those sharings, those discussions of not only what has happened but how we are feeling and dealing with the situations, have led to a much deeper friendship, level of trust, level of understanding.

Teams wrote about taking courses together, taking trips together, and becoming part of each other's family. Team members felt their friendship was a model for their students and was reflected in the students' behavior. Many team members commented that their students benefited from seeing people working together in harmony. Students were able to observe adults solving problems, negotiating, and just plain having fun together. As Violet said with a smile, "One of the little girls complimented us because she liked the way we played together."

There are several things about working with teams that make me view my job differently. For example, it's definitely harder in hiring, because with single teachers, you can hire for specific qualities, and they can go into their classrooms and shut the door. I think that as administrators, we probably face more demands and challenges from the staff than we did in the traditional setting. When the teachers come to us with a problem or suggestion, they've already worked through it; when they come in here, they pretty much have their backs together. That's why on major decisions, we might take twenty-four hours; we don't give them one immediately. In the old days, one-on-one like it used to be, it was different. Now a lot more needs to be considered. And there's more strength on their part with three or four team members. It requires a clear philosophical view on the administrator's part to respond to situations appropriately. It's hard. It's fun.

Ken Vaughn
Middle School Principal

CHAPTER

8

How Principals See Team Teaching

Knowing how to deal with uncommon situations that arise unexpectedly is a large part of a school administrator's job. Generally speaking, he or she has a point of reference—a peer or available research—that provides something more concrete than gut instinct to rely on when making decisions in new situations.

Not so with team teaching. When the mandate came down from the Nevada legislature in 1990 that all first-grade classrooms would have a fifteen-to-one pupil-teacher ratio, school adminstrators were among those most surprised. They had no research to read because this team teaching phenomenon was generally unheard of in education circles. They had little or no time to collaborate, brainstorm, and plan with peers or their staff members. They often had no choice but to institute team teaching in their schools and work it out as they went along.

Yet the teachers turned to their administrators for answers, support, and solutions. Many administrators rose to the occasion in fine fashion, while others seemed to flounder.

Their descriptions of team teaching were varied and interesting. Each site administrator had definite ideas about what constituted the important elements of a team. One focus group of eight administrators from elementary, middle, and high schools produced the following list of what team teaching can or should be:

- A partnership.
- Planning toward a common goal for an individual child.
- Two or more people working with a common group of kids.
- A system with a name, kids, and teachers.
- Four-teacher teams (middle school).
- Special education "push-ins."
- Working in the same space at the same time.
- A symbiotic relationship with multigraded teams.
- Teachers with similar backgrounds and experience.
- Teachers with common philosophies and teaching style.
- Gender balance.

The first three items are key elements in all team teaching at all grade levels; the others are variations that depend on the specific configuration.

Forming Teams

The first year, the principals created teacher teams using a variety of methods—teacher choice, sociograms, drawing of straws, seniority, and everything in between. The result was some exemplary teams and some absolutely disastrous ones. Learning from experience, the principals formed their teams quite differently the second year.

The principals in our focus group listed the following as necessary conditions for forming successful teams:

- The teachers need to be committed to the idea.
- The principal should help teacher teams communicate with each other and resolve conflicts.
- When the principal must designate a team, he or she should be sure the members are compatible and amiable.
- The principal should see to it that support is available throughout the year.
- The principal should provide team members time to plan, both before they begin team teaching and along the way.

Just as teachers have a plethora of teaching styles, principals' administrative styles vary greatly. Many of the concerns expressed by teachers—about evaluations, planning time, communication difficulties, lack of support—seemed to occur more or less often depending on the style of the school administrator.

For example, principals who met with teachers before they went into the classroom to observe a teaching team seemed to have fewer problems evaluating the individual teachers within the team. Peter shared these thoughts about teacher evaluations and team teaching:

> With the limited experience that I have had this year in evaluating teams, I would change my approach in the future. I tried to evaluate team members as I have in the past, observing each individual member presenting a somewhat "canned" lesson so that I could see the teachers' individual strengths and weaknesses, and how they deal with children individually.
>
> I have discovered that this is an unreal circumstance in a team. In order to truly evaluate a member of a team, I need to see how each member supports the other(s), how one's weaknesses can be supplemented by another's strengths, and how as a team they can be more effective than perhaps they are individually.
>
> Perhaps some teams might feel uncomfortable about this way of evaluating; then it is my responsibility to win their confidence and show them that they are not going to be judged by their partner's performance but by how they individually contribute to the success or failure of the teaching process in their classroom. After all, the bottom line is whether the students learn and have a good experience; whatever process is used to get them to that point is the one that should be evaluated.

Another key difference lay in how a principal views communication and his or her role in the process of team-member communication. Martha recalled how she and her team teachers had a meeting at the beginning of the year: "We talked about what team teaching might look like. I just asked them to let me know if I could help in any way. Several teachers have given me written notes specifically on what they would like me to do."

In addition, throughout the year, she sent written notes to the team teachers just to say, "How's it going? Why don't we meet on such-and-such a day to talk?" She continued, "We try to meet once a month or month and a half to see how it's going. They say, you know, it's tough, but we're working through it."

George made sure he visited the teaching teams as a unit; he tried to share news with all members of the team at the same time. He thought it was vital that the teachers in a team feel they have equal value in his eyes. He also asked them, "How am I doing? Can I do anything to help?"

Roger has an open-door policy and encourages his teachers to come in and talk any time. In addition, he tries to be in the classrooms as much as possible.

Principals' Concerns

Principals had some very specific concerns about team teaching:

- How to ensure flexible hiring practices within the school district and enlist teacher support for those practices.
- What to do when a team is in trouble.
- How to allow teachers to bow out of a team gracefully.
- How to evaluate individual teachers within a team.
- How to evaluate the team as a team.
- How to include non–team teachers.

These concerns bring up a new set of issues. How do non–team teachers perceive team teaching? Some grumbling invariably occurred about the discrepancy in numbers of conferences held and report cards prepared and about the extra time team teachers received for planning. We concluded that it is vital for all staff members to be made aware of the extra demands placed on team teachers.

Benefits to Children

Without exception, the principals we interviewed and talked to in focus groups believed that if the team was working properly, the benefits to students were overwhelming. One principal said that if he had a choice, he would place his own child with a team rather than with an individual teacher.

Principals enumerated the following benefits team teaching offers children:

- Two sets of professional eyes observe each child, and decisions regarding help and retention are made with twice the experience.
- More than one teaching style gets the point across to more children in a better fashion.

- There are more "good days."
- Small-group instruction, remediation, and enrichment can be provided more easily.
- Discipline can be handled quickly without disrupting classroom routine.
- Teachers are more eager.
- The departmental walls in middle school and high school are broken down.
- There is a better sense of community in the classroom.
- Students have two people to bounce off of, to react to, to offer reinforcement.
- Students have an excellent example of a positive adult social relationship.

How Can Principals Help Their Teachers?

The principals said that they helped team teachers however and whenever their teachers requested such help. Martha and several other principals arranged to take the students out of the classroom for P.E. or some other group activity so that team teachers would have that time to plan. (Both Martha's new and seasoned teams decided to forgo the extra planning time the second year because they felt they didn't have enough time with their students.)

George assisted his teachers by promising, "If it isn't working for you as a team, I'll find a way to release you from the commitment. Just give me one year and give me your best shot." Knowing they had that "out" lent an extra measure of success to his teams.

Principals at the middle and high school levels believed their main support was scheduling a common prep period for the team teachers so that planning time was assured. All the secondary administrators interviewed felt that voluntary buy-in of the team-teaching model was mandatory for success.

All the principals we talked with advocated more in-depth staff development at the district level. They strongly urged that workshops be offered—during the teachers' workday—in communication skills, conflict resolution, and thematic teaching strategies. In addition, they felt teachers needed release time just to talk. What's working? What's not working?

The following letter of support, encouragement, and suggestions from a school principal is a concise, informative, and thoughtful description of team teaching.

> To whom it may concern:
>
> I am writing this letter in reference to team teaching and how I, as an elementary school principal, might address the issue now that I have been through this experience with two teams for one year.
>
> Because of some experiences that I have had this year (mostly positive), I have become convinced that once the teams have been selected, there are some things that need to take place within the teams before actual teaching begins. One of the most crucial parts of this process is for the team of teachers to take time to talk together concerning possible difficulties that might arise, as well as basic teaching philosophy (including discipline).
>
> I think if I were to start a new team, I would outline some very

basic areas that I feel need to be discussed between them. I may or may not include myself in the discussion phase, but I would make certain that both parties understand the importance of such a discussion, and I would also make certain that a date and time had been set for such a meeting before I would excuse myself. For that discussion between team members to be successful, it must be understood by all that honesty and full communication must exist between parties. I would also stress that they should think about some of the following areas: (1) how each teacher disciplines children; (2) how each teacher is going to share or not share the children; (3) how regularly scheduled activities (such as calendar, lunch count, etc.) are going to be run and who is in charge of them; (4) what the work ethic is of each teacher in the team: do they want to work together on weekends? how late do they want to work after school? what outside commitments does each member of the team have? what kind of family support does each member have? (5) how conflicts are going to be resolved between team members; (6) how team members will accommodate different teaching styles; (7) what the best way is for team members to communicate feelings when there are issues to be resolved; (8) how the team is going to keep peace in the family. There are certainly many other issues to look at, and there needs to be some sort of ongoing evaluation by the team of where they are as a team and whether any new issues need to be discussed.

Some other issues that you as a principal may want to look at during the course of the year are (1) how to make sure you treat team members as individuals and not always as a member of a team; (2) how to provide planning time during the school day; (3) how you will conduct observations and evaluations; (4) how teachers that are not part of the team can be made to feel part of the process; (5) how conferences with parents will be handled; (6) whether there will be a lead teacher; if not, how will you (and they) communicate with the team? will all decisions be joint decisions?

I believe that in order for teachers to work as a team they must be able to communicate their desires and feelings with one another. Many teachers go into this situation thinking that because they are professionals it will all work out. What they forget is that they are also human, and while eventually they may be able to read one another's mind, initially they won't be able to, and so they must be able to communicate with one another.

Team teaching situations can be very beneficial to students and teachers alike. It is important that members of the team feel successful in dealing with the situation, so that children can feel successful. The principal can set the tone, and he/she may even have to mediate when there are differences (and there will be), but the best people to solve these problems are the members of the team themselves.

Good luck in your efforts.

Mutual Concerns

Teachers and principals had many of the same concerns about team teaching: on-task teaching, evaluation, support, and communication. All teachers have a working relationship with their administrator, and the degree to which team teaching was successful often depended on the degree of interaction between those involved.

Substitutes

The substitute teacher is a hot issue among team teachers, principals, and district personnel. Monica declared, "I don't think it's right that the principal can pull one of us to cover another teacher's class. If it's an emergency, I can understand it. But it has the danger of becoming a habit." This became the cry for many teachers and administrators alike, especially when substitutes were scarce districtwide and administrators were told to "pull a team teacher to cover."

Over and over again, teachers and principals talked about team disposability. Some team teachers preferred to carry on alone when the other member of the team was out. Yet many others felt this made the team expendable: was this really a team-teaching situation or was it shared teaching? And substitutes were not always available even when both the teachers and the principal had agreed to call for one. Our study showed that team teachers and principals need to decide ahead of time the best solution for their own situation and that the district needs to provide some direction when a substitute is necessary.

Support

Two of the most exciting side effects of team teaching are the innovation and creativity that occur when two teachers can brainstorm and solve problems together. Yet these benefits can be jeopardized by lack of understanding and support from the principal. Shannon said:

> Our principal is now open to ideas like this. At first he shrunk back when I told him some of our ideas. Now he says, "I think you guys could probably do some of that stuff." He trusts us.
>
> Next year we're going to keep a lot of special education students in our classroom. We're both certified special ed teachers, so we can adapt to meet their needs. We'll do their IEPs [Individual Education Plans] in the classroom also. We wanted to do it this year, and he said he didn't think it would work, so we asked for next year, and he said yes. We think we proved ourselves—he thinks we adapt enough to meet their needs! So that's kind of nice.

Nearly all of the concerns and complaints seemed to revolve around lack of communication between the team teachers and their site administrators. Eldris shared:

> I often felt like my principal dealt with teachers mostly by crossing his fingers. When he heard about past problems or problems in other schools, I could see him mentally fanning himself with a "Whew!" and patting himself on the back in congratulations. He never inquired into problems we had as a team, but he never was one to seek out bad news. In his defense, I must say that I don't think he had a great deal of information or practice in dealing with teams, and I did always have the sense that he wanted everything to work out and that he truly appreciated the efforts we made on behalf of our students and our school.

Our study showed that team teachers had begun to realize that the administrators had little, if any, training to guide them in this new endeavor, and that they, the teachers, must make their feelings and needs known to their supervisors. And the principals have realized that they are the ones responsible for opening the lines of communication with the individual teachers and with the teams.

In closing, here is Eldris's "wish list for my principal":

- Do encourage experimentation and questions.
- Do let teams know how to seek help.
- Do provide training in basic interpersonal skills.
- Do provide resources and continually seek new ways to foster team growth and interteam sharing.
- Do try to minimize changes in other areas. As teaming is a major change, and too much change is difficult, avoid as many other changes as you can in our school.
- Do find out from other principals, and let us know, what other schools/team members are doing successfully.
- Do share with us any new information that becomes available to you as soon as possible.
- Do make contingency plans for a variety of outcomes so we know we can count on you for back-up when plan A fails.
- Do provide more feedback than usual to encourage the extra efforts made by teachers as individuals and as team members.
- Do share your feelings/reactions to problems we must jointly solve. It builds confidence and trust during stress. However, put it on an equal basis with our feelings and reactions; don't make it the focus for everyone else.
- Don't take resistance to district policy personally and become defensive. Please just listen and empathize.
- Don't allow teams to become rivals. Encourage cross-team collaboration.
- Don't delegate and duck out. Empowering teachers is not the same as dumping on them; when a new idea fails, we can share the blame and criticism for its demise.
- Don't feel like you're the Lone Ranger out there having to deal with this. We're all in this together, and we appreciate the support you give us.

Team-taught classes are great. I was fortunate enough to participate in World Cultures, a combination history and English class instructed by two top-notch teachers. Together, they kept sixty of my fellow peers and myself occupied and energetic about learning for two hours straight. We were often less than willing to learn—more interested in attending to our ever important social issues—yet we somehow managed to learn the material. It amazed me how sixty sophomores could learn not only as peers, but as friends. But looking back, I realize this was no accident, simply a side effect of the style in which we were taught. We usually worked in small groups—reading together, discussing together, and learning together. My thoughts were open to new ideas and points of view. In short, we learned new and better ways to think.

The lessons taught spanned far beyond English and history; we learned how to work with others as well as to think for ourselves.

Keith Knight
High School Student

CHAPTER

9

Through Students' and Parents' Eyes

Our research group wanted to hear from the students themselves what being in a team-taught classroom meant to them. We went about this is several ways: children in third-grade classes were asked to reflect and write on what it had been like for them in previous years having two teachers instead of one; middle school students were asked to participate in a focus group and complete individual surveys about their experiences both with a team of teachers and with a team of students; and high school students involved in team-taught interdisciplinary classes were interviewed on video about their experiences in these classes.

The benefits educators use to defend innovations often come in standardized forms, such as test scores, attendance, and grades. However, it was important to us to capture a sense of the daily experiences children have in a team-taught classroom and how they internalize or make meaning of this experience. In this chapter, therefore, we rely heavily on the actual voices and words of the students as they described their year with team teachers.

Not all of the benefits of team teaching identified earlier (see Chapter 7) were important to the students. As might be expected, educational assessments were not germane to any of them. In addition, neither elementary nor high school students commented specifically on their peers as teachers. Elementary children did not comment on the value of two teachers' perspectives and expertise in terms of instructional practice. They focused solely on the value of having another adult to go to.

More of Everything

All three groups of students cited more of everything—more personalities, more talk, and more fun—as one of the main reasons team teaching worked for them. A number of middle school students mentioned the opportunities to talk that team teaching provided. For example, one student responded:

> I really like my team. I like all the kids and the teachers. I like the times we meet because I'm learning a lot. I like how we do "inside/out-

side," a technique used by the teams to help people get out in the open with their feelings.

Many elementary students emphasized their enjoyment of teams, often focusing on "more fun" as their reason for viewing teams positively, as well as mentioning learning more from the presence of "more teachers." A comment from one third grader reinforced the observation that team teaching presents a unique opportunity for children to see two adults communicating positively with each other. In this rare case of a male-plus-female team (we had only four male teachers in our study), the child noted, "Girl and boy together, like you and Mr. G. Both of them were nice."

Almost half of the high school students who viewed "more" as a positive aspect emphasized the relational aspects of the team: two compatible adults who liked each other and kept the interest of the class. For example:

- "They'd joke around, made learning fun, not boring. Towards the end, we would clap."
- "They picked the teachers really well—they worked together well. They added spunk and humor."
- "You don't get bored listening to one the whole time."

Personal Attention

The younger the student, the more likely they were to list personal attention as a reason they valued team teaching. Nearly half of the third graders in our study commented on the help they could receive, either for personal needs or with their schoolwork:

- "A teacher can help with personal things."
- "They can get to you faster if you need help."
- "While one teacher is busy, the other can help you."

The attention factor was also seen as a means for teachers to stay in control. As two students noted:

- "One can teach and the other can make sure people are doing their work."
- "You can go on a train trip—with two teachers, you have more control."

Working Together

For middle and high school students, the collaboration of two or more individuals within the classroom made the biggest impact. Seeing two adults negotiate a series of complex interactions throughout the day was very powerful. As these middle school students indicated:

- "I thought it was nice the way one teacher could go to the other for ideas."
- "All the teachers working together on the same stuff makes it easier to understand."

Middle school students couched the benefits of seeing their teachers collaborating and working together in language that referred to having a sense of family, having a group to belong to, and learning how to get along with—even like—different people:

- "I like teaming because you don't have just one friend in the whole school. You have a team of friends."
- "Working together will help me later in life."
- "Teaming is like a second family. You can trust one another."
- "You have someone to count on, to trust."
- "You have to get along with or work with people you don't like."
- "Someone teaches you how to work with others, and get along with others, and care about other people's feelings."

The concept of belonging to a group as a facilitative aspect of learning was also noted by high school students:

- "It wasn't a class, it was a family. We got involved in shaping the class."
- "We did a lot of things together—the family aspects. We got to care about each other, made some great friendships."
- "You're forced to work with people, get to know them on a more personal basis."
- "I got to know a lot more people in a shorter time, and had to interact with people we didn't normally get to know."

The high school students' comments about collaboration also mentioned the depth of knowledge they could explore in the context of groups and the importance of communicating with a group of people to understand themselves and the subject matter better. Here are four examples of the responses we received:

- "It opened me up. It's two hours with a lot of people—you have to learn to communicate. I used to despise oral reports, but my group helped me structure my reports and made learning that much easier because it was in a relaxed atmosphere."
- "You get more involved. I learned a lot through groups, went more in-depth, not cut off really quickly."
- "I liked it because you get group work a lot more. You get three to six people's input. You think about things you didn't think about before."
- "Group activities brought out a lot more creativity in the students because we had competitions; and what would normally be boring, we used creative formats to present."

Added Perspectives

Another important dimension of team teaching for middle and high school students was the added perspective another teacher brought to the subject matter. Many middle school students expressed this simply: "understanding more things" or "learning better." Occasionally students would describe this aspect of teaming in more detail:

- "Knowing more information is available and getting to know more thoughts and ideas."
- "One of the teachers always put it into a perspective I could understand."

The high school students reported that learning two different subjects, when combined, became a new whole, something greater than the parts. One student reported that reading the biblical story of Ruth in three different versions as a literature activity gave him a "greater sense of the world." Another student described the synergy this way:

> We got more into the culture of what we were studying. It really tied everything in when you got to see both sides. Usually, in history, you study what happened; usually, in English, you read.

Still another had this to say:

> There's always someone that knows what's going on—a specialist in each field. Right in the same lecture the two fields are merged through the teachers' presentation. There's two viewpoints on almost everything instead of one teacher's perspective. The cultural and the historical are presented; I learned a lot about my opinions because a lot of it is group work. With two teachers' opinions you can learn to make your own opinion.
>
> It's not like you have one teacher for one hour. It's two teachers for two hours. The class becomes a new class. There's not a turnaround at the break. A big part of tests are essay questions. The English teacher helps you write well about historical facts, and when the subjects are separated, it's not as clear because the teachers don't know what you're doing in other classes.

An offshoot of the merging of two disciplines and the fact that two teachers were aware of the requirements each was imposing on students for his or her subject matter was the team's willingness to balance out the teaching requirements to achieve the best learning outcomes for students. A student commented about this two-hour block of team teaching in the high school:

> With both teachers in one class you get the respect of the teachers for the assignments the other has given, and you can balance out and spend the time you need on each individual assignment, and you have enough time to finish assignments, making time for more activities instead of just reading and analyzing.

Though in general having two or more teachers in the room was seen as beneficial, some teachers feared that some students might see an opportunity to play one teacher against the other, something children often do with their parents. This was not, however, borne out by the students. High school students did not mention it; middle school students occasionally saw the idea of more than one teacher as a distinct "disadvantage" of team teaching:

- "One can teach and the other can watch and make sure people are doing their work."
- "You have a better chance of getting caught."
- "More teachers to get yelled at by and you get in trouble more."

The Middle School Perspective

When responding to our questions about the benefits of team teaching, the middle school students kept listing the advantages and disadvantages of being involved with their peers in a team instead of focusing on their teachers, as we had intended. We finally realized that we were trying to impose a framework for team teaching that did not fit their circumstances.

In this middle school model, team teaching embraced a core of approximately ninety students with seven teachers. For these students, team teaching was a social and academic enterprise, and team teachers included anyone whose "shoulder they can lean on," whom "they can work with" "in one room to teach or learn." They could not, and understandably should not, separate team teaching from their team experience. Team teaching in middle school embodied a sense of equity and intimacy that characterized the learning process. Student teams spent as much as two or three years together, and a majority of their school time involved carrying out projects of interdisciplinary learning that built on the separate subject-matter classes they took with about one-third of their team. Once we understood their orientation and their definition of teams and team teaching, we asked them to list the advantages and disadvantages of team teaching. This is the list they produced:

Advantages

Learn to cooperate.

More fun to learn.

Meet different people.

Get to do a lot of activities out of class.

More flexible time. Able to include more things.

Variety and consistency are key elements of the team.

Opportunity to address issues with teachers on a regular basis (inside/outside group meetings).

Friday projects as team.

Field trips are fewer, but more fun as a team.

Disadvantages

More homework, class assignments, notes.

More to keep track of—teachers and classes.

Always have to plan ahead; responsible to others.

Not getting the homework needed to be prepared for high school.

Could cause more conflict because around each other a lot.

Have to learn to get along with people you may not like.

Exposed to boring lectures. More teachers; more things to do.

Less chance of getting away with things.

Being compared to other teams.

Hard to concentrate with more best friends.

The final advantage they listed was perhaps the most touching summation of the middle school students' concept of team: "No one's better than all of us."

A Standing Ovation from the Teachers at Home

When team teaching was introduced into the Washoe County School District as a way to meet the legislative mandate and as a mechanism for restructuring the middle school, many thought parents would be wary of this innovation. Indeed, teachers and principals throughout our study noted the parents who expressed concern about whether team teaching was indeed a good solution for their children.

As a conclusion to our study, we decided to solicit input directly from the parents. We asked a number of our team teachers to distribute surveys to parents in their classes (see Appendix C). We received a total of forty-one surveys from parents, the majority representing children from first and second grades (ten and twenty-eight, respectively). Only 7 percent of those responding expressed a negative reaction to their children's experience with team teaching. Their disapproval centered largely around classrooms that were divided into two groups taught side by side, with very little integration. Their comments included the following:

- "Makes class too big—more noise in class, less room for students."
- "The classes were taught in one room, divided in half by a board. I feel it is a bad setting. First, the kids talk to each other more, poke the other kids, or copy from each other's papers. Second, it's difficult for them to learn with another class going on at the same time."

Some of the parents who felt there were more disadvantages than advantages to team teaching nevertheless qualified their responses with ideas that sounded very much like those of the teachers who felt that team teaching is a relationship that works best when two teachers enter into it equally and responsibly and with respect for each other:

- "When it works, it works well. There are two teachers to help and work with the children. When the teachers complain and criticize there is double the negative feedback."

- "This was a good team. Not all teams work and not all teachers can avoid the temptation of leaving the room or doing paperwork while the other teacher has thirty students all to herself."
- "If the team works well together, it is great. But not all teams work well together."

We can learn a lot from these few comments about guidelines for establishing a team and working together as a whole class. We can also better understand what parents valued about team teaching and recognize that this information can be useful in setting the proper tone for parents who have just learned that their children will be part of a team-taught class.

The parents' positive comments were similar to those expressed by the students; however, parents were much more likely to focus on the perspective and experience that two adults in the classroom could offer children or the division of children into smaller groups for more one-on-one attention:

- "Two different personalities to watch and learn from."
- "Each teacher has her own way, and I think kids learn a lot."
- "There is a combination of ideas and attitudes—a wider range of teaching and learning."
- "I think two teachers have different ideas, and maybe when what one teacher uses doesn't work, the other teacher's ideas can help a student."
- "Flexibility for the student to be able to relate to one in some areas and to the other in different areas."
- "He feels better with two teachers because he feels he's learning more that way."
- "It would seem he may get twice the attention and support for learning."
- "It allows for more flexibility in the way smaller groups can be arranged by one teacher, while the other can lead the class in another activity."
- "The slower children didn't hold up the rest of the class, since the child could get some special time with one teacher while the rest of the class continued with their learning."
- "My child receives more one-on-one education, and two in the room keeps the children supervised better."

The parents who responded to our survey and the number of positive comments teachers shared with us indicated that team teaching was received much more positively than negatively by parents. Parents expressed appreciation that they were able to meet with two teachers during conferences to validate what they had heard, that their children had continuity in instruction when one teacher was out sick, and that their children received special attention when they needed it:

- "My son was pretty lucky. He had two really good teachers."
- "Our compliments to Mrs. Terry and Mrs. Ashby for a job well done!"
- "My child did really well this year. I was really impressed with the teachers!"
- "Keep up the good work. Daniel has improved immensely."

APPENDIX A
THE STORY OF OUR STUDY

What we accomplished together, not one of us could have done alone.
Fran Terras

Several factors combined to bring our group together for our study of team teaching: first, all of us shared a natural curiosity about the teaching-learning dynamic and wanted to seek out the most effective ways to teach; second, we had all participated in a Northern Nevada Writing Project summer invitational institute; and third, each of us was searching for still another avenue for professional development that would provide direction, stimulation, and formalized association with colleagues with similar concerns. A collaborative project was just what we needed to both continue our individual professional development and draw attention to the benefits and value of teacher research: working together to address concerns that spanned grade levels, curriculum issues, and politics.

The Pilot Study

It all began with Tamara Durbin Higgins. At one of our meetings during the fall of 1990, Tammy, a first-grade teacher, described the experiences she was having as a team teacher and her and her partner's plan to begin keeping a journal. Several others in the group—teachers at levels ranging from kindergarten through high school—then shared their experiences as team members as well.

We began by asking questions: What is team teaching? What makes a team successful? How can we look at this complex phenomenon in a way that will enable future teams to enhance their experience as team teachers in our school district? We finally decided we would study successful teams—what they looked like and why the teachers in those teams considered themselves successful. We knew that we could not investigate all aspects of team teaching. Rather, we agreed to search for information from a limited sample that would enable principals and teachers alike to create teams with improved odds of being successful.

Method

We began in March by sending letters to all 112 teachers in Washoe County who were currently involved in team situations, asking them if they felt the year so far had been successful and if they would be willing to be interviewed. We received replies from 62 teachers, 54 of whom said yes to the interview. A little overwhelmed by the positive response, we realized we needed to narrow our study.

We limited our targeted teachers to first-grade teams, then prepared a list of 25 prospective interviewees representing a variety of socioeconomic areas, years of experience, and team-placement methods. Sometimes only one member of a team participated, sometimes both. We then generated a set of sixteen questions (see Figure 1) centered around the following issues:

1. How the method by which the team was formed affected the team situation.
2. The physical adjustments teams had to make to accommodate the team situation.
3. The teaching and management philosophies of team members.
4. The methods teams used to plan instruction.

Armed with the questions, tape recorders, note paper, pencils, and interest, we interviewed the teachers on our list.

Results

In general, all us us came away from the interviews impressed by the teachers we talked with and keenly aware of the wide variety of their styles, backgrounds, and experiences. The quality they shared was evident: an unflagging commitment to the educational and personal success of their students. The teachers never let the distress that might have been part of team teaching color or threaten the well-being of students in their classrooms. In addition, we found that a sense of commitment was instrumental to the success of the team. Regardless of the variety of situations, the diversity of teaching styles, and the differences in preparation time and planning, team teachers who were successful were so because they were committed to making the situation work. Another key element was the degree of choice a teacher had about whether and with whom she or he would team teach.

Many more issues related to team teaching emerged during this first phase of inquiry: the metaphor of a marriage; the reference to team teaching as a powerful model for students who seldom saw two adults communicating and relating in a consistent fashion (other than their own parents, if they lived in households with two parents); and the acknowledgment that it became easier over time to negotiate differences in classroom management and philosophies, even though the issues did not disappear.

All our findings pointed up the necessity of communication skills and administrative support. Most teachers had been trained to be in charge of their classroom and make instructional decisions within, at most, the confines of the district's and school's curriculum guides and time schedules. The issue of maintaining a physical and psychological space in conjunction with another teacher was not one with which teachers, whether novice or veteran, were well acquainted.

Our pilot study generated a great deal of interest. In fact, our findings were used by a state legislator during the 1991 session to document the positive side of team teaching, which may have contributed to the legislative vote to continue the mandate.

The Second Study

Responding to the interest our pilot study generated among study participants and district personnel, we decided to continue our investigation. Our preliminary results provided a framework for a more in-depth and systematic inquiry that, in turn, could serve as the basis for a practical book about team teaching by and for teachers, offering multiple models and describing successful teams.

We took what we had learned from our original data and developed categories that represented the full range of possibilities in each of the areas we intended to study further. In other words, we translated our overall picture of the issues related to team teaching into manageable summaries that enabled us to survey, in our new study, the total population of team teachers in Washoe County.

We expanded our investigation to include teams from all levels of education and with varying configurations, because we were most interested in team teaching as a professional alternative rather than as a legislative mandate. Our study included elementary teams, "push-in" teams, middle school teams, and secondary teams.

Our sample of 59 teachers was voluntary, gleaned from respondents to a survey (see Figure 2) mailed to the 377 team teachers in the district, as identified by themselves, administrators, and colleagues. From among those who agreed to participate, we systematically selected a stratified sample using criteria of school location, grade level, number of years team teaching, choice in team teaching, and perceived success as a team. Few of our participants were male, which limits our findings but also perhaps raises some interesting questions about feminine perspectives and experiences with team teaching.

As noted earlier, we discovered that the term *team teaching* has multiple definitions and configurations, and that it involves more than simply two teachers working in a certain space limited to four walls. One team member, expressing ideas common to many others, wrote:

> Team teaching is two or more people putting their minds together to form one large community of thirty students. A successful team shares common goals, all of which benefit the partners and their students. Teams communicate, cooperate, support, give and take, provide role models, serve as "think tanks," and find humor in themselves, coworkers, and students. Teaming is like being married. Along with all of the above, you share responsibilities, make decisions together, and spend a heck of a lot of time together!

In the early stages of our study, the participants answered questionnaires designed to reveal background information as well as planning and classroom management issues (Figure 3). Throughout the study, they attended focus group meetings, kept journals, and took part in two interviews. Toward the end of the study we asked each participant to complete a follow-up survey (Figure 4). Finally, we invited some team teachers to join us for three days in August 1992 to write the vignettes you see throughout this book. As much as possible, we attempted to gather firsthand information from the team teachers and to maintain the integrity of their perspectives.

What We Discovered

The ideas in this book generally provide a positive picture of team teaching because that was a prevalent theme in our sample and one of the first assumptions that led us into this inquiry. Early on, our research group sensed that successful teams would be positive about their experiences; however, team teaching was not a positive experience for everyone. (Those feelings are addressed specifically in Chapter 6, although they are dealt with elsewhere as well.)

Our Assumptions

Three major assumptions about team teaching framed the first questions we asked the teachers in our study:

1. Team teaching is a positive, legitimate option for teachers.
2. Having the choice of whether or not to team teach is essential to doing so successfully.
3. Team teaching is a teaching dynamic worthy of study outside of the legislative mandate.

We also had a host of ancillary assumptions. First, we assumed that in order to be successful, team members would need planning time to get to know one another. Second, teams that shared the same philosophies about curriculum and children would be more likely to be successful than those with divergent views. Third, good communication is perhaps the most critical element for a successful team.

Under the closer scrutiny of our second study, we began to question some of the assumptions we held about team teaching, although we saw this transformation of our thinking as a strength rather than a weakness. The areas we had chosen to study were, in fact, important areas for successful team teachers, but we learned that these areas were dynamic and could not be broken down into the neat categories we had laid out in our pilot study.

Difficulties

Because we did not have much experience interviewing and transcribing tapes, we were unprepared for the number of hours required to transcribe the interviews, conduct focus group meetings, and keep track of and sift through all the data. We were overwhelmed with the amount of physical work.

We cared so much about this project and were so committed to both the teacher-researcher process and one another that at times we all worried that the physical and emotional strain would take its toll on our friendships and professional alliance.

It did and it didn't. Part of being a teacher-researcher is becoming a reflective practitioner. So while we dealt with the difficulties we encountered, at the same time we continued to grow and change as teachers, researchers, and people. Often throughout the three years of our study, we commented on how appropriate it was that our twelve-member research team was engaged in a study of team teachers. At times, the mirrorlike quality of our study and our own team process made our heads spin.

Collaboration Breeds Commitment

Often, we began our meetings with a short journal-writing period to help us focus on the important developments each of us had discovered or reflected on since the previous meeting. Sharing our entries, we would find that others in the group had experienced similar revelations—and then the discussion would be off and running. It was through these rich, meandering discussions that we came to new insights. We met every other Tuesday to talk, analyze data, and write. We shared concerns, conflicting data, and personal experiences as team teachers. And we moaned about the difficulty of it all.

We found ourselves bound to one another in this discovery process. We learned that no one of us could have undertaken the study alone, although there were times when each of us felt like bailing out. But collaboration continued to breed commitment. And from the beginning of our experiences as teacher-researchers, we commented frequently that if it had not been for our shared sense of humor, we would not have been able to accomplish our goal.

Fulfilling a Commitment

As we put these final words to paper, after hundreds of hours of editing and revision, we reflect again on the tremendous number of hours put in by every member of our group. The stories contained within each chapter, and our weaving of them to offer this whole picture of team teaching in Washoe County, Nevada, moved us deeply. And as reading upon reading of the text brought us closer to the whole, we were struck again by the enormous growth each of us has experienced in the years we have worked together as a group, interviewing, transcribing, and writing.

It has been tiresome, difficult, and taxing. But still we remain a cohesive whole. We have gone through marriages, divorces, babies, job changes, house changes, career changes, cancer, and many other major life changes. But we have seen this project through to the end. Our collaboration did breed commitment.

Questions for Interview on Team Teaching

1. How long have you been teamed with your partner?
2. How was your team formed? How do you feel about the way your team was formed?
3. What qualities are most important in a teammate?
4. How much time did you spend with your partner before the school year began? Was this time funded in any way?
5. How did you use this time? What did you talk about?
6. How much class time do the two of you spend simultaneously involved with students?
7. In what ways do you structure that time? What kinds of activities happen during this time?
8. How have you adjusted the physical environment of the classroom for the team situation?
9. How do you plan your lessons? Is there a scheduled time that you do this together?
10. How has planning changed as the year progressed?
11. How and when do you talk? Is there another way you communicate besides talk?
12. Have there been conflicts within the team? If so, how did you resolve them?
13. What have you discovered about each other's teaching philosophies? How did you come to that understanding? Have you had to make adjustments or compromises?
14. What question would you like to answer that we forgot to ask?
15. Has team teaching affected the way you view your role as an educator? If so, how?
16. What is team teaching to you?

Figure 1 *Questions for Interview on Team Teaching*

Survey Sent to 377 Team Teachers

Dear Colleague:

We are a group of teacher-researchers interested in studying team teaching at all grade levels. Our focus will be on strategies and conditions that enable a team to work effectively. We would greatly appreciate your completing this brief questionnaire. Your responses will be kept confidential.

Date: ______________________________
Name: ______________________________
School: ______________________________
Subject taught: ______________ Grade level taught: __________
Partner's name: ______________________________
Subject taught: ______________ Grade level taught: __________

1. How many years have you been a team teacher?
   How long have you been with this partner?

2. Why do you team-teach?
   Had to?
   Wanted to?
   Explain.

3. How were you matched with your partner?
   I was placed.
   I chose my partner.
   Explain.

4. Has team teaching been successful for you?

This year	*Previously*
Yes	Yes
No	No

   Explain.

5. Did you have any planning time with your partner before the start of the school year?
   Yes
   No
   Explain.

6. Did you participate in any training to prepare you for team teaching?
   Yes
   No
   If yes, please list what and when.

Figure 2 *Survey Sent to 377 Team Teachers*

7. Would you be willing to participate in our study?
   Yes
   No

The teacher-researcher group plans to share the summary of this study with interested teachers. Please add any comments or questions that might help us as we begin our study.

This project is being funded by the Walter S. Johnson Foundation and will involve about 60 interested teachers and principals, K–12. We plan to interview these teachers and principals as well as establish and facilitate focus groups for the participants. We recognize that you are the expert on team teaching and believe that this voluntary project will allow you an opportunity to share your expertise and knowledge with others. We appreciate your time and input.

Sincerely,
Tamara Durbin, Director
Deborah Loesch-Griffin, Consultant
Gaylyn Anderson, Dissemination Coordinator
Mike Gazaway
Carol Harriman
Margaret Hill
Liz Knott
Susan Martin
Karen McGee
Joan Taylor
Fran Terras
Ellen Williams

Figure 2 *(continued)*

The Questionnaire

Background Information

1. How long have you been teamed with your present partner?
   Current school year only (1991–92)
   Currently and 1990–91 school year
   Longer (circle one) 3 4 5 6 7 years

2. Indicate below the manner that best describes how your team was formed.
   Partner decision
   Principal selection
   Random pairing
   Interview selection

3. How much time did you spend preparing for team teaching before the school year began?
   No time (partnered at the last minute)
   Time prior to the beginning of the school year
   In-service class with partner
   In-service class without partner

4. If you spent time with your partner prior to the start of the school year, which of the following was discussed? Check all that apply.
   Physical arrangements
   Teaching philosophies
   Curriculum development
   Getting acquainted
   Other

Philosophy

1. Circle the number that indicates the degree to which you and your partner agree about the following classroom matters (1 = strongly disagree; 5 = strongly agree):

Teaching style (i.e., product vs. process, whole language vs. phonics)	1	2	3	4	5
Expectations of students	1	2	3	4	5
Teacher-student interaction style	1	2	3	4	5
Time commitment to teaching	1	2	3	4	5
Planning	1	2	3	4	5
Discipline	1	2	3	4	5
Homework	1	2	3	4	5
Classroom neatness	1	2	3	4	5

2. Name three qualities that you think are most important in a teammate:

Figure 3 *The Questionnaire*

Planning

1. When do you plan?
   Special release time scheduled by principal
   Prep period during school time (i.e., music, library, regular prep period)
   After school or before school prep time
   Hours over and above 8:30–3:30

2. How much time do you spend planning outside of school time?
   ——— hours per week.

3. Generally, how do you and your partner plan for class time? Select the one that describes how you most often plan.
   Divide curriculum responsibilities
   One partner does the majority of planning
   Plan together
   Each teacher plans for his/her own students

4. When you compare planning time in September to now, which of the following best describes how your team's planning has changed?
   Increased time planning together
   Decreased time planning together
   Not much change

5. Rate the benefits (5) or drawbacks (1) of having another professional in the classroom with you.

Being able to brainstorm ideas	1	2	3	4	5
Motivation	1	2	3	4	5
Sounding board	1	2	3	4	5
Kids have access to two role models	1	2	3	4	5
Collegial support	1	2	3	4	5
Sharing physical materials	1	2	3	4	5
Being aware of peer in the room	1	2	3	4	5
Personality differences	1	2	3	4	5
Sharing control/leadership	1	2	3	4	5
Integrating many ideas into available instructional time allocated	1	2	3	4	5
Working with different teaching philosophies	1	2	3	4	5
Other	1	2	3	4	5

Management

1. Which of the following best describes your team teaching style most of the time?
   Dual-directed teaching—both are giving direct instruction to the whole group interactively

Figure 3 *(continued)*

Alternating as lead teacher—giving direct instruction, partner acting as helper, reinforcer, etc.
Both are teaching small groups same subjects
Both are teaching small groups different subjects
One teacher generally assumes lead role, partner as helper

2. About how much class time do you spend simultaneously interacting with the students?
   More than 90%
   More than 50%
   Less than 50%
   Other

3. Do you view yourself as a teacher of 30 (whole class) or 15 (half class) in terms of the following areas?

	Whole class	Half class
Grading		
Discipline		
Conferencing		
Parent letters		
Bookkeeping		
Other (please explain)		

4. What physical needs have been created as a result of team teaching? Check all that apply.
   Extra storage for teachers
   Extra storage for students
   Two teacher desks
   Arrangement of student desks
   None
   Other (please explain)

Figure 3 *(continued)*

Follow-Up Survey

We are in the final stages of writing up the results from our study on team teaching and wanted to touch base with you once again to find out your current situation. Please take a few moments to answer the following questions, and add any last words you might have on the experience of team teaching. Thanks again for sharing information with us, and we hope you'll have a chance to read about the findings from our study in our upcoming book.

ID#:____________________________ Date: ____________________

1. Are you still in a team teaching situation?
   Yes
   No
   If yes, please complete 2-3.
   If no, please go to 4.

2. Are you still team teaching with the same person?
   Yes
   No
   Comments:

3. Are you team teaching with someone new?
   Yes
   No
   If yes, what are the reasons you are with a new partner? Please check all that apply:
   ___ Changed school site
   ___ Changed grade level
   ___ Needed a change of partner
   ___ Mutual agreement to split
   ___ My partner left:
      ___ Retirement
      ___ Relocation
      ___ S/he needed a change of partner
   ___ Principal suggested break

Figure 4 *Follow-Up Survey*

4. If your team ended this past year and you are no longer team teaching, what were the reasons for this ending? Please check the *one* response that best describes your ending.
   ___ Overage
   ___ Mutual agreement to split
   ___ One partner left:
      ___ Retirement
      ___ Relocation
      ___ Incompatible with partner
   ___ Team burnout
   ___ Principal suggested break
   ___ Tired of situation—team burnout or partner burnout
   ___ Other (please describe)

5. If your team was split or you left team teaching, would you consider team teaching again later?
   Yes
   No
   Why?

6. If still team teaching, do you see yourself continuing in this situation beyond this year?
   Yes
   No
   Why?

This is the last word we'll ever ask you on team teaching (maybe, probably): Is there anything you'd like to say at this point or anything you said last year that you'd like to change or comment on? Please feel free to share any last insights or reactions to team teaching. (If you need more space, please write on back.)

Again, thanks to all of you for your patience and continued support throughout this project. We never could have achieved our goal without your cooperation.

Figure 4 *(continued)*

APPENDIX B
CHECKLIST OF TEAM TEACHER ISSUES

Team teachers have reported that discussing and then making decisions about the following issues before beginning to teach together help to prevent conflict later and make the team more efficient right from the start.

Classroom Space, Materials, and Time

- Work spaces?
- Storage?
- Furniture?
- Desks/tables?
- Teacher desks?
- Materials, books, supplies?
- Which materials are mine, which are yours, which are ours?
- Partitions/room dividers?
- Centers?
- If school doesn't provide what we need/want, how will we get it?
- How can we set aside several hours of joint planning per week?
- What content should each of us teach?
- What content should be divided?
- What content should be taught jointly?
- How will we keep records? One or two grade books?
- Who grades which papers?
- What grading system?
- Lesson plan book?
- Personal neatness preference?
- Work outside of school hours?
- System/organization?

Needs/Values/Philosophy

- Tolerance of noise level?
- Personality strengths/weaknesses?
- Learning style?
- Feelings about teaching?
- Phonics? Whole language?
- Teacher training or staff development I've had?
- Schedule as related to my out-of-school life (i.e., have to pick up own kids, taking classes, etc.)?
- Parent conferences? (Yours? Mine? Ours?)
- Things about my teaching I'd like to be better at?
- Social interaction between us?
- Things we have in common?

- Things that make us different?
- Affection?
- Humor/Drama?
- Cooperative learning?
- Grouping?
- Level of expertise? (Subject matter? Teaching strategies?)
- Who teaches what?
- Interactions with children?
- Spontaneity/asking for help?

Classroom Management

- Disciplining?
- Rules/Expectations?
- Consequences?
- Classroom routines (i.e., lining up for recess etc.)?
- Movement within classroom?
- Constructive criticism?
- Communication with parents?

APPENDIX C
PARENT SURVEY ON TEAM TEACHING

Dear Parent(s):

For the past three years a team of teacher-researchers has been studying team teaching in the Washoe County School District. We are very interested in learning some of your experiences as a parent of a child who is being taught by a team of teachers. Please take a few moments to respond to this survey and return it in the self-addressed stamped envelope. Your responses will be kept confidential. Summaries of parents' responses to this survey will be included in the final report of our findings on team teaching.

Please focus on this year's team teaching experience.

Grade your child is now in: __________

1. When you first learned your child would be in a classroom with two or more teachers, what was your response?
   ____ Negative ____ Neutral ____ Positive
   Please feel free to comment:

2. Have you had a parent conference with your child's teachers?
   ____ Yes ____ No

3. How did they run it?
   ____ As a team
   ____ Only one teacher met with me

4. If you met with *both/all teachers* during the conference or during any other time of year to talk about your child and what they were doing in the classroom, what was it like meeting with two teachers instead of one?

5. Does your child talk about both teachers or does he or she usually focus on one when talking about school with you?
   ____ Both ____ Only one

6. What has been your child's reaction to being in a team-taught class?
   ____ Negative ____ Neutral ____ Positive
   Please feel free to comment:

7. How do you feel *now* about team teaching?
   ____ Negative ____ Neutral ____ Positive

8. Would you say there are more advantages or disadvantages for your child in this type of teaching situation?
   ____ More advantages ____ More disadvantages
   Please explain:

Thanks again for your time in completing this survey!

APPENDIX D
A QUESTION POSED TO A TEAM TEACHER

Are there new ways you have learned to relate to others because of team teaching? Please describe.

Team teaching was not an activity either one of us had been taught to do. Frequently, the team teacher must ask him- or herself, "What must I do, or what must be done, or how can I best communicate, to help the team stay alive and function at its full potential?" It seems to me that the need to ask oneself such a question has, in fact, led to growth in how to relate to others.

The following seem to be the ways my teammate and I relate that may not necessarily occur in any other working relationship at school, at least not to such a great extent:

1. When differences in opinion arise, do not commit yourself quickly and unconditionally to one point of view; instead, take time to step back to think about all of the options, and then make a suggestion and work out the decision together.
2. When differences arise, one technique that is useful is to "bite one's tongue." Often, stepping back from the situation has given me time to think about my own feelings and how to respond without worrying about one particular person or group's being angry or disappointed, but concentrating on what is best for all concerned.
3. Take the full value of the other person's words and philosophy into account with each decision. In order for the team to work, each member must respect the other as a professional and as a person.
4. Always weigh the good of the group when considering the good of the individual. That is, consider a compromise that can be worked out between the teammates that will benefit the class as a whole rather than being totally invested in one's own ideas.
5. The very nature of our program creates a need for some of our students to be mainstreamed for a specific subject, such as math. This has underscored our need to relate to the mainstreaming teachers with respect, courtesy for their style of teaching, and belief in the value of the other teacher's program and in your mutual student's abilities and quest for improved skills.

ABOUT THE AUTHORS

Born and raised in the San Joaquin Valley of California, **Gaylyn Anderson** has spent much of her life in Reno, where she earned her bachelor's and master's degrees in English at the University of Nevada, Reno. A teacher for twenty-one years at Reed High School, she is also a writing consultant with the Northern Nevada Writing Project (NNWP) and the University of California, Irvine Writing Project. She co-authored the Washoe County School District (WCSD) middle and high school writing guides, has published articles on teaching writing and literature, and has directed two literature institutes for teachers. Her love for the classroom is reflected in her work as a teacher-researcher on the classroom as a community of learners. Her love for the ocean and the outdoors is reflected in her other interests—traveling, photography, sailing, and poetry. She lives in Reno with her husband and two daughters.

Dr. Nancy M. Doda, who contributed the foreword for this book, was the first classroom teacher to keynote the National Middle School Association's annual conference. A team leader on an interdisciplinary team, she has taught sixth-, seventh-, and eighth-grade English and reading in an exemplary, multi-graded middle school. Much in demand across the country as a conference speaker and workshop leader, Nancy is on the staff at National-Louis University's Washington, DC site where she works with the DC public schools in their middle school reform efforts.

Michael Gazaway has been a teacher for seventeen years, having arrived late in the game. "I was twenty-nine when I had my first classroom," Michael recalls. "When I did begin teaching, it was in a very small community of 350 people located in northwestern Montana, where I was an intermediate grade teacher. I moved to Reno nine years ago. I teach in a school that is located in the center of Sparks. The contrast between where I came from and where I am now is incredible, to say the least. I have a real interest in literature and use what I have learned about it to teach my reading classes. Nine years ago I entered into an experiment in team teaching. It involved combining remedial reading students and identified low readers in one classroom with the remedial reading teacher and the regular classroom teacher. Our textbooks were novels. My partner, Fran Terras, and I pooled our talents and found success beyond our expectations. The experience was invaluable." Michael is currently teaching sixth grade at Lincoln Park Elementary and recently completed his master's in education at the University of Nevada, Reno.

A native Nevadan, **Carol Harriman** has been a student or a teacher in Nevada schools for most of her life. After receiving a B.A. at the University of Oregon, she returned to Elko, Nevada, and taught there for six years. Then for seventeen years she taught English and speech at Reed High School. Carol is currently the English Program Coordinator for the Washoe County School District. She received a master's degree in Speech Communication at the University of Nevada, Reno, in 1980. Since that time, she has been an active consultant in the Northern Nevada Writing Project, serving as its director from 1989 to 1992. She is also involved in a portfolio group and has been a teacher-researcher for seven years.

Tamara Durbin Higgins always knew she would be a teacher. "From the time I first smelled a fresh ditto clean off the machine, I knew education would be my niche," says Tamara. "That was first grade at Mamie Towles Elementary School in Reno. I still lament the passing of blue, inky fingers and sneer inwardly when the copier jams. But teaching is much more to me than those smells, or the feel of warm hugs from my first- and third-grade students. Teaching is researching, collaborating with peers, and ongoing learning for myself. I have taught for fifteen years, all but one of those years in the first grade. My time with six-, seven-, and eight-year-olds has taught me much, most importantly that there are no easy answers and that the hardest day of teaching is still more worthwhile, more energizing than a day spent doing anything else. I am proud to be a teacher, a teacher-researcher."

Margaret Hill lived the first six years of her life in Needles, California. "However, the last seventeen years have been spent in Reno at Clayton Middle School enjoying the diversity that middle school students bring to the classroom," she said. "Being in the teacher-researcher group has enabled me to examine my role as a professional and the methods I use in hopes of getting specific end results. My working with this group of extremely talented teacher-researchers has greatly enriched my life, both on a professional and a personal level. Associating with professionals who have enthusiasm for students and faith in what they do is inspiring and helped me find new faith and hope in my own classroom." Margaret has recently retired and is traveling extensively throughout the country.

Elizabeth Knott, born in Occupied Japan and raised in Saline County, Missouri, began teaching journalism and writing in Santa Monica in 1969 after graduating from the University of Southern California's School of Journalism. From there, she taught at a Garden Grove, California, junior high and at Carson City High School in Nevada. "In 1977," she says, "I came to Reed High School in Sparks, Nevada, joining an amazing group of innovative, dedicated educators. The conditions, atmosphere, and my philosophy along with my school's came together allowing me to grow, grow, grow. I enjoy learning at California Association of Teachers of English (CATE) conventions, from the Northern Nevada Writing Project consultants, and with the team teachers whether interviewing, 'focus grouping,' or sharing students. My family life centers on raising three teenagers:

my poetic daughter, my karate-focused philosophical son, and my Pop-Warner dynamic son."

After years of wanderlust and world travel, **Deborah Loesch-Griffin** has come to call Virginia City, Nevada, home. "Although I rarely spent a tenure beyond three years in any place or position, the journey brought me many insights and gifts into the different ways people—even in this country—live. Consequently, my own life is far from traditional, although one glance at the space I occupy with my two sons and husband might make any farsighted reader question this claim. I'm a working mom and a career wife by society's standards, and I'm neither of these by mine. I am a woman trying to make a difference in my own life first—to make it worth getting up, hassling with school lunches and laundry, and to bring my children some sense of hope and joy in their own journeys. 'Making a difference in lives' is a theme I've embraced since I was a child. Whether it be a strong and enduring friendship, counseling a distressed child or family, or developing programs to serve a community or school need, I have dedicated most of my waking hours to this task." Deborah owns and operates Turning Point, a small consulting firm she established in 1990 that specializes in school-community partnership development and program development and evaluation.

Originally from Latrobe, Pennsylvania, **Susan Martin** graduated from Indiana University of Pennsylvania, then began her teaching career on the eastern shore of Maryland. After spending three years there, she moved to Nevada in 1979. She has been teaching English at Reed High School for seventeen years and is currently co-director of the Northern Nevada Writing Project. Sue lives in Reno with her husband and two children.

Karen McGee has been the Reading Coordinator for the Washoe County School District for the last seven years. "In that position, I have been allowed into K–12 classrooms throughout the district to teach model lessons focused on innovative practices for teaching reading/language arts. Between 1975 and 1990, I taught all the primary grades in three different elementary schools, co-directed the Northern Nevada Writing Project, and taught several reading/language arts classes at the University of Nevada, Reno. "I learn by talking with others, so I love working with other professionals who help me discover what I know and what I need to learn to become a more efficient teacher. Perhaps my greatest passion is for teaching. I hope I live long enough to become the teacher I aspire to be." Karen is married to a judge who also writes children's books and is the mother of three grown children.

Joan Taylor is originally from San Francisco, California, and received both her bachelor's and master's degrees from the University of Nevada, Reno. She and her two sons reside in Reno, where she is currently teaching fifth grade. Joan has spent most of her teaching career in middle school grades. Having been in a team-teaching situation herself, as well as researching and documenting other team teachers' experiences, has given her the opportunity to study the subject from a unique perspective.

Fran Terras is a native Nevadan who was raised in the small towns of Goldfield and Tonopah. For as long as she can remember, she wanted to be a teacher. She was one of those children who ran a school every day. She grabbed the neighbor children, stray animals, relatives and, when all else failed, stuffed toys. She has been teaching thirty-six years (if you don't count all of the years of youthful practice). Her experience includes twenty-seven years as a remedial reading specialist, four years as a sixth-grade teacher, three-and-a-half years as a fourth-grade teacher, and two years as a third-grade teacher.

Ellen Williams comes from a long line of elementary teachers, but she never wanted to be a teacher until she spent one day in a second-grade class. Twenty-three years later she is still enjoying every day of her chosen profession. Except for a two-year stint teaching in the Department of Defense Dependents Schooling Program in Germany, all of her years teaching have been spent in Washoe County School District.